Harriet Beecher Stowe

Updated Edition

Twayne's United States Authors Series

David J. Nordloh, Editor

Indiana University, Bloomington

TUSAS 42

HARRIET BEECHER STOWE
(1811–1896)
Photograph courtesy of the Picture Collection, the Branch Libraries,
the New York Public Library.

Harriet Beecher Stowe

Updated Edition

By John R. Adams

WITHDRAWN

Twayne Publishers
A Division of G. K. Hall & Co. • Boston

Harriet Beecher Stowe, Updated Edition
John R. Adams

Copyright 1989 by G. K. Hall & Co.
All rights reserved.
Published by Twayne Publishers
A Division of G. K. Hall & Co.
70 Lincoln Street
Boston, Massachusetts 02111

Copyediting supervised by Barbara Sutton
Book production by Janet Z. Reynolds
Book design by Barbara Anderson

Typeset in 11 pt. Garamond
by Huron Valley Graphics, Inc., Ann Arbor, Michigan

Printed on permanent/durable acid-free paper
and bound in the United States of America

Library of Congress Cataloging-in-Publication Data

Adams, John R., 1900–
    Harriet Beecher Stowe / by John R. Adams.—Updated ed.
        p.   cm.—(Twayne's United States authors series ; TUSAS 42)
    Bibliography: p.
    Includes index.
    ISBN 0-8057-7532-3 (alk. paper)
    1. Stowe, Harriet Beecher, 1811–1896—Criticism and
interpretation. I. Title. II. Series.
PS2956.A6 1989
813'.3—dc19   88-26563
                                                         CIP

Contents

About the Author

John R. Adams received his degrees from the University of Michigan and the University of Southern California, where his major fields of interest were aesthetics, the history of philosophy, literary criticism, and American literature. He has visited many parts of the United States and has lived and taught in Ohio, Michigan, Alabama, Washington, and California. His latest position was professor of English and chairman of the Division of Humanities at San Diego State University.

Professor Adams's first published essay, "A Provincial View," appeared in the old *Saturday Review of Literature* when Henry S. Canby was editor. Since then he has written briefly on diverse subjects from Milton to Henry James and at greater length on regional books, Harriet Beecher Stowe, and Edward Everett Hale (also in Twayne's United States Authors Series). He has also served as newspaper correspondent and book review editor. Although retired from teaching, he maintains membership in several philological societies and continues writing on literary subjects.

Preface

In the years since this book was published in 1963, Harriet Beecher Stowe has been examined and reexamined by many kinds of experts; consequently my book is different from what it was in its first edition. Its primary purpose, as a balanced survey and evaluation of Stowe's published writings, remains unchanged. Its secondary purpose, as a guide to current as well as earlier opinion, introduces new material. A book could be written on Stowe and her critics, and in fact a book has already been written on *Uncle Tom's Cabin* and its critics. This is not such a book, but I have duly noted the discoveries and very interesting speculations of the current experts; and I have referred to them as liberally as my space and energy have permitted. I confess that I have read through and sorted out well over a hundred books and articles written since 1963 in the hope of finding them useful to my readers.

Among the best of these, as described in the Selected Bibliography, I recommend two for their happy combination of scholarship and readability: Edward Wagenknecht's *Harriet Beecher Stowe: The Known and the Unknown* (1965) and Thomas F. Gossett's *"Uncle Tom's Cabin" and American Culture* (1985). Several permanently valuable reference books are the bibliographical compilations of Margaret Holbrook Hildreth (1976) and Jean W. Ashton (1977), as well as the anthology of essays edited by Elizabeth Ammons (1980). A bibliographical study, *The Building of "Uncle Tom's Cabin"* (1977), by E. Bruce Kirkham, is a model for method and results.

Biographical information about Harriet Beecher Stowe has increased, mainly through institutional archives where collections of manuscripts have become open to examination. The Beecher family has been scrutinized collectively and individually. As to Harriet herself, family letters add depth and color to a story already familiar in outline; a few are so private as to disclose the bedroom conduct of Harriet and Calvin. The most inclusive of these accounts is Milton Rugoff's *The Beechers* (1981), in which the sections about Harriet constitute almost a full-length fully documented biography. The book about the older sister, *Catharine Beecher* (1973), by Kathryn Kish Sklar, is also important; and Robert Meredith's book on Edward Beecher, *The Politics of the Universe* (1968), shows that the elder brother was more than casually helpful to his sister.

Numerous studies have viewed Stowe's work in connection with broad social tendencies. Her gradually changing ideas about religion, race, and womanhood have been shown to parallel those of large groups of her contemporaries and she has been seen as a representative American of her time. Among the books that have contributed to the enhancement of her reputation, or at least have made her seem a more interesting person, the best are Ellen Moers's *Literary Women* (1976); Mary Kelley's *Private Woman, Public Stage* (1984); Ann Douglas's *The Feminization of American Culture* (1977); and Jean Fagan Yellin's *The Intricate Knot* (1972).

As the cultural significance of Stowe's writing has become clearer, close examination of her work has stimulated the production of technical monographs and articles more appealing to professional scholars than to the public in general. Written for specialists on varying levels of aesthetic sophistication, they range from straightforward arrangements of facts into new patterns, like Josephine Donovan's *New England Local Color Literature: A Women's Tradition* (1983), to high-level literary theory that staggers the imagination, as in Philip Fisher's *Hard Facts: Setting and Form in the American Novel* (1985). Several unpublished but excellent doctoral dissertations have been produced as laboratory work.

At the other extreme, Stowe's name was mentioned in newspapers nationwide in connection with a new dramatic version of *Uncle Tom's Cabin* performed on television in June 1987. Popular radio lectures (by Leslie Fiedler, to be sure) have found their way into hardcover publication as *The Inadvertent Epic* (1979). Of little or no importance, but amusing, is Stowe's walk-on appearance in an expressionistic novel by Ishmael Reed, *Flight to Canada* (1976), in which she makes an anachronistic long-distance telephone call on business for Jewett Brothers. "I need a new silk dress." Also amusing and marginal is an article by a clinical psychiatrist in *American Imago* (1983) in which Stowe the patient suffers violent verbal attacks of sibling rivalry, childhood replacement, beating fantasies, and masochistic tendencies, yet survives and is pronounced sound and able to utilize her conflicts.

Evidence of interest in Stowe is a reversal of the earlier neglect. When I began studying her writing seriously, about fifty years ago, *Uncle Tom's Cabin* was her only book in print. The *Writings* of 1896 and other individual volumes from 1843 to 1878 were out of print: she was on the road to oblivion. A large part of her work had never been collected or reprinted or cataloged. My first task, probably assigned by my friend Louis Wann, chairman of my doctoral committee at the University of Southern California, was to ferret out, read, and assimilate these uncollected writings. We were surprised at how many I found, stories and essays from youth to old age, in magazines, newspapers, and prefaces. Of course I missed a few, but I am confident that I was the first (and probably only) person to attempt this not-so-heroic task. Unfortunately for her reputation, I found no absolute literary gems, but I uncovered enough sound workmanship to prove that Stowe was no lucky one-book author but a skillful, versatile journeyman writer. I continue to believe that her almost forgotten writings, collected and uncollected, throw light on her major accomplishments. The titles of the obscure pieces I found have been absorbed into Hildreth's bibliography, where they can be easily located; but my reward came as long ago as 1940, when I received my doctor of philosophy degree, my dissertation being the first on Stowe to be accepted by an American university.

Between 1940 and 1963, when Sylvia Bowman gave me the opportunity to write the first edition of this book (for which I shall be permanently grateful), the notable new books and articles on Stowe included Forrest Wilson's *Crusader in Crinoline* (1941); Charles H. Foster's *The Rungless Ladder* (1954); Edmund Wilson's essays in *Patriotic Gore* (1962, from his *New Yorker* articles as early as 1955); and James Baldwin's 1949 *Partisan Review* article, "Everybody's Protest Novel," which initiated further protests and controversies extending over years.

Aside from attacks on "Uncle Tomism," most of the later writing on Stowe has been favorable to her. Tomism itself has been separated from her as readers of her book have observed for themselves that Stowe's Tom is presented clearly as a strong character, a martyr to his principles, not a weakling unwilling to protect himself. Writers on Stowe's feminism have also become tolerant of her lukewarm concern for women's rights. Women of several generations have extolled Stowe, from Annie Fields, who wrote the best biography of its time (1898); they have dissected her character and writing, as in Constance Rourke's brilliant essays (1927); and current highly trained academic women scholars find more in Stowe's version of womanhood to pity or praise than to ridicule or condemn. Above all, current criticism treats her as a significant writer entitled to serious attention.

John R. Adams

Chronology

1811 14 June, Harriet Elizabeth Beecher born, daughter of Lyman and Roxana Beecher, at Litchfield, Connecticut.

1816 Roxana Beecher dies.

1824 Harriet's earliest preserved school composition, "Can the Immortality of the Soul Be Proved by the Light of Reason?" Moves to Hartford, attends and teaches school at the Hartford Female Seminary, run by her elder sister.

1825 Composes a tragedy in blank verse, "Cleon" (unfinished).

1832 Beecher family moves to Cincinnati, Ohio.

1833 Harriet's first published writings, in *Western Monthly Magazine*.

1836 6 January, marries Calvin Stowe (born 1802); September 29, first children, twin girls, born. Antiabolitionist riots in Cincinnati.

1849 Cholera epidemic in Cincinnati, causing the death of the Stowes' infant son.

1850 Return to New England, when Calvin Stowe receives appointment to the faculty of Bowdoin College at Brunswick, Maine. 8 July, Charles Edward born, the last of Harriet and Calvin Stowe's seven children.

1851 5 June, first installment of *Uncle Tom's Cabin* in the *National Era,* followed by book publication in 1852.

1852 Move to Andover, Massachusetts, when Calvin Stowe joins the faculty of Andover Theological Seminary.

1853 First of three visits to Europe (others in 1856 and 1859), as described in *Sunny Memories of Foreign Lands* (1854).

1856 Publication of *Dred,* Stowe's second novel.

1857 Eldest son, Henry, dies by drowning. First contribution to the *Atlantic Monthly* (vol. 1, no. 1).

1859 Publication of *The Minister's Wooing,* Stowe's first completed New England novel, after serialization in the *Atlantic Monthly.*

1862 Publication of *The Pearl of Orr's Island,* after serialization in the *Independent.*

1863 Lyman Beecher dies.

1864 Move to Hartford, Connecticut, after Calvin Stowe's retirement from teaching.

1869 Publication in the *Atlantic Monthly* of Stowe's sensational article on Lord Byron's incest, followed by an expanded version in book form, *Lady Byron Vindicated* (1870). Publication of *Oldtown Folks,* her most substantial novel of New England, without prior magazine publication.

1873 Publication of *Palmetto-Leaves,* descriptive sketches in praise of Florida, her winter residence from 1868 to 1884.

1878 Publication of *Poganuc People,* her last novel, after its serialization in the *Christian Union.*

1886 6 August, Calvin Stowe dies at Hartford, Connecticut.

1889 First official biography of Harriet Beecher Stowe, by Charles Edward Stowe, her son; and first unofficial biography by Florine McCray.

1896 1 July, Harriet Beecher Stowe dies. Publication of *Writings,* in sixteen volumes, followed by an official biography (1898) by Annie Fields, a friend of many years.

Chapter One

Early Years

Harriet's Parents

The essence of Harriet Beecher's early life can be expressed in the word *subservience*. In the early nineteenth century, by law and by custom, males dominated politics, business, the professions, and the family. In traditional conservative households like the Beechers, the father's dominance was undisputed, and wives and children, especially girls, were fortunate if the patriarch was affectionate in his despotism. Harriet Beecher, one of the more fortunate, was also inevitably a victim of the sex discrimination that spread throughout American society.[1]

From the years of her earliest recollection Harriet had cause to brood over her position in the Beecher family. She was the youngest daughter and the seventh child of Roxana Foote Beecher, Lyman's first and favorite wife, who, having given birth to nine of Lyman's children, had contentedly died. Of the eight children who remained to mourn their mother, the eldest was Catherine and the two youngest Henry Ward, two years Harriet's junior, and baby Charles.

Though dead and buried, Roxana was not forgotten. Her character as submissive wife, idyllic in its perfection, could not have wielded in life more influence over her children than it did in their memories. As family legend, she gained power through Lyman's marriage, two years later, to Harriet Porter, a woman born to be respected but hardly equal in human kindness to the lamented Roxana. Throughout his life, and in spite of a literal impossibility, since at her death he was too young to have retained any recollections of her, Henry Ward stoutly maintained that Roxana had been the greatest influence on him. Harriet held the same belief, though her own memories were but a scanty three, and two of them were of rebukes to the children for making too much noise and for eating tulip bulbs under the misapprehension that they were onions.[2]

The surviving parent, the Reverend Lyman Beecher, was the type of man in whom energy is easily mistaken for genius. A powerful personal-

ity, the head of the family was a fiery evangelist for the Lord and the
Beechers. Within his home Lyman was a bully of the worst stripe, a
benevolently intentioned and systematically complete bully. It is difficult to know which alarmed his children more, the sternness with
which he ordinarily treated them or the periods of capricious high
spirits that were vented upon rather than shared with them. If Lyman
Beecher customarily spared the rod, the reason was that he wielded
more powerful instruments of torture, the most successful being dialectic and hellfire, which, as a disciple of Jonathan Edwards, he was adept
at unleashing. In his logical battles with his children, which he considered admirable discipline for them, he loved to befuddle and humble,
never permitting them privileges because of tender years. As a result,
Henry Ward confessed that he had never felt at ease with his father, he
had always been so conscious of the restrictive vigilance of the old
Calvinist.

In the Beecher family religious instruction was no weekly formality,
for indoctrination was carried on continuously through daily family
worship. Lyman knew exactly what he demanded of his children; he
insisted that the boys become ministers and carry on his work, as
eventually the seven did who reached maturity. The girls' futures concerned him less, as there was little a girl could do in those days except
marry, preferably a preacher. Consequently, or so Harriet was convinced, beyond terrifying his daughters with the dangers of hell, he
neglected them, and much of her girlhood was saddened by the slight
esteem in which she seemed to be held. Lyman's proud declaration that
she was a genius, a statement made when she was about seven years old,
could have satisfied her only in part, as he immediately qualified it by
the wish that she might have been a boy. Feminine genius, as much as
was needed in the Beecher household, was already manifest, in the
father's view, in the oldest daughter, Catherine, twelve years Harriet's
senior.

Undoubtedly, in the lives of the Beecher children there was much
happiness and jollity, as on the regular nutting excursions when their
father romped about like a boy and Harriet was allowed to dress and
play like her brothers. In her later stories, Stowe often dwelt upon the
advantages of a New England upbringing, but she did not even then
forget the neglect she suffered as child and female. For her there were
only fleeting escapes from the benevolently harsh rule of a father who
did not know his own blighting strength.[3]

Sister Catherine

Nor was the second decade of Harriet's life to be less restricted than the first. A difficult enough period for young Christians of the Beecher tradition, the time of conversion, it was more than normally hard for Harriet, who at twelve years had been sent from the family home at Litchfield, her birthplace, to Hartford to be placed under the direction of her stern twenty-three-year-old sister. An orphanage would have been as homelike as the Hartford Female Seminary, for in Catherine the father's bullying instincts were reproduced and underscored. She undoubtedly loved her little sister, whose life she made miserable.

For Catherine, poor soul, more than a word of extenuation is needed. Endowed with intellect beyond most men's, and her father's favorite daughter as his first child, she was less the victim of discrimination than of a vindictive fate. At a suitable age she had become happily engaged to a Yale University professor who had died in a shipwreck before undergoing the ritual of a Presbyterian conversion. Although an idealist with exemplary habits, he was considered in the Beecher household to be nonetheless irretrievably damned, unless he had squeezed into heaven by a last-minute declaration. Of this there were unfortunately no evidences, nor did the young man's character point in the direction of strict Calvinism. The Beechers were crushed, even young Harriet suffering sympathetically. Catherine remained near mental collapse for years. In this morbid state of mind she continued until she was saved by a grim determination, since personal happiness was denied her forever, to do good for others.

Catherine consecrated herself to the cause of improving female education. Using a legacy from Professor Fisher as a nucleus, she gathered funds to establish the Hartford Female Seminary, and Harriet became the first victim of her experimentation. A gorgon in her later years, Catherine was in early womanhood a formidable creature, unfitted by either temperament or training for the work she undertook. Self-admittedly she had been poorly educated at Miss Pierce's school, of which she spoke slightingly, and she was no doubt incapable of teaching some subjects that she essayed, such as Latin, for which she was coached two weeks. Her self-confidence was ample, for her rule was to regard herself as acting precisely as God, had he been a female educator, would have chosen to act. That viewpoint solved all her difficulties, she said, and dispelled all her doubts.

Though in these early years Catherine must have taught superficially in her struggles with chemistry, rhetoric, logic, history, algebra, and natural philosophy, as well as Latin and moral philosophy, she was from the first a perfect disciplinarian. When Harriet was discovered writing a poetic tragedy, Catherine bade her abandon such foolish vanity and set her to studying Bishop Butler's *The Analogy of Religion, Natural and Revealed, to the Course and Constitution of Nature.* As soon as Harriet was able to assist with the teaching, Catherine kept her so busy that the younger girl became dangerously nervous, groaning and crying in her bed half the night and laughing loudly and irrationally throughout the day. Her work was a burden to her; she felt that her life was being wasted in caring for little kindergarten animals.

Harriet's Conversion

Simultaneously, during this decade of Harriet's teens, while the sister overbore, the distant father—who had left his pastorate at Litchfield in 1826 and settled in Boston to do battle against the Unitarians and Harvard University—pursued her through the stages of her exhausting conversion to Christ.

The basic outlines of Lyman Beecher's Calvinism are shocking and frightening to the intellectually immature. For him, Jonathan Edwards was its chief exemplar and expositor. According to this greatest of divines, as his disciple interpreted him, man was by nature actively evil, in spite of being endowed with will sufficient to withstand evil. Man was free to be good, certain to be bad, and undoubtedly fit after this turbulent life only for those everlasting hellfires that a just God had provided for man's future abode. Escape? Through human nature there was none. Hope? One alone, the mercy of a pitying God for the favored among a wicked people. Assurance? None whatever. To feel one's soul safe was, to a man of Beecher's creed, a pitiful delusion. Whenever he discovered members of his flock flirting with the dangerous idea, he hurried to pay pastoral visits warning against this suggestion of the devil.

As no one has pointed out more clearly that Harriet, in novels written much later, within this system compounded of sin and hellfire, a system too easily labeled Puritanism, multitudes of distinctions could be drawn. A rich dialectic exhilarated the theologians, providing encounters of wit that were the joy of acute minds such as Lyman Beecher's. For a child like Harriet in her teens, however, the harsh simplicity of the outline was all that was visible. She knew only that her salvation depended on being scared out of her wits.

Later, when the diversion of traveling and the pleasure of young companions had restored apparent happiness, so that she ceased to wish for an early death, she could still look back yearningly upon the memory of her mother and imagine that if Roxana had lived she would have spared her daughter much of the useless agony of salvation. Reading the Book of Job was not a comforting substitute. The display of God's power and strict justice appalled her, and her only consolation was her faith in the mercy and compassion of Jesus.[4]

In surviving the ordeal of conversion, she became convinced that Jesus loved her in spite of the mortal sins her father declared lay within her, and with Jesus she found the perfect companionship lacking in daily life. Her work as teacher was a vexation that symbolized the world, from which she retreated to the arms of the great lover. Against all her father's principles, she never again doubted her salvation; but she remained for many years weak in body and subject to periods of petulance and irritability. With every reason to feel the opposite, she set about conscientiously trying to develop a spirit of kindliness by remembering her happy hours and allowing the others to slip from her memory.

Cincinnati and Marriage to Calvin Stowe

For eight years Harriet had been separated by her Hartford bondage from the head of her family. If there had been no relief in this separation from her father, neither was there immediate comfort in their reunion (1832), when the Beechers moved en masse from Boston to Cincinnati. On the contrary, the change restored two masters over her, for she was to continue as assistant to Catherine in a new female college while living in the home and, hence, under the control of her father, now president of the eminent but insecure Lane Theological Seminary.

Cincinnati, the border settlement of mushroom growth that Lyman had glowingly described as the London of the West, impressed the Connecticut-bred girl as only an uncouth town with the same humdrum routine of the female college. The father might excite himself with visions of saving the entire West for Jonathan Edwards, but the daughter was absorbed in annoying questions of quills and papers dropped on the floor or of drinking in the entry. Her exhausted mind, she felt, was sinking to its death. Thought and emotion alike pained her, and she passed her time in listless vacancy, busied with trifles.

At this time of crisis, meditating upon Mme de Staël's *Corinne,* a popular romance that had found its way into the Beecher household, she reflected almost philosophically on the emotional starvation of America. Morbid and deep feelings, when repressed, she recognized, reduce a human soul to only dust and ashes. Thought might have dawned seriously upon her had she not succeeded in arousing herself from such melancholy reflection through the dual escape into what may be flatteringly called Literature and Love.

She began to write magazine sketches, and she accepted a marriage proposal from a lonely widower. Both moves worked to her advantage eventually, but marriage was the more productive immediately. If she had anticipated independence from family domination by marrying Calvin Stowe, she was to be grievously disappointed, for Calvin, though he did not imperiously impose his will upon Harriet, as her father and sister had done, had his own effective way of regulating her conduct. The first children, twin girls born on 29 September 1836— the marriage had occurred on 6 January of the same year—were followed by five others. Within four years of the wedding ceremony four children had been born to them; and six of their seven offspring, the last born in 1850, survived childhood. Harriet was bound more closely to household tasks than ever before, and there is evidence to suggest that she sometimes regretted having married the good soul out of sympathy with him over the death of his first wife.

That pathetic fate, household martyrdom, was in store for her; and except for her poverty she might have elevated herself to that station. Since there was money in the world, she resolved to help support the family—by writing. The Beechers had long complained about the poverty suffered by the Lord's servants. The children, Henry Ward in the van, grew tired of living from one Sunday collection to the next; and after Harriet's marriage the lack of money became the most intense goad to commercialization of her abilities. When she said, in her later years, that she began writing because she and Calvin needed money, the statement was as nearly true as its simplicity permitted.

The husband, although a charming and amusing man in hours of relaxation, was nearly ten years her senior and of a predominantly solemn cast of mind. In youth he had been a sober, earnest student; and his later experiences as teacher of Greek and theology, at Dartmouth and Lane Seminary, had made him mentally more nearly her father's contemporary than Harriet's. He was a sincere servant of the Lord, President Lyman Beecher's first professorial convert to the idea of saving the West for orthodoxy. For this piety she respected and honored him, as well as for his broad scholarship in philology, a subject unfortunately of no great interest to her. By far the strongest tie between them at the beginning was their common affection for his dead wife, Eliza, who had also been the daughter of a distinguished theologian—a love so enduring that throughout the many years of their lives, on every anniversary of her birthday, Calvin and Harriet might have been seen hand in hand before her portrait, communing with her.[5]

From the first Harriet pitied this sad, learned man, without becoming passionately excited by him. On the morning of her marriage she wrote in italics to a girlhood friend that she felt *nothing at all.* For years she was not enthusiastic about Calvin. After the birth of the third child she wrote an old friend that she could speak well of her marriage *after all;* and this admission was about as far as she would go publicly. In 1841 she felt herself destined to an early death, and she wavered between her devotion to her writing and to her children. In her weakened health—she was at one time near prostration from the death of her brother George—rainy days would reduce her to an extreme in which she became so sick of the sour smells of meat, milk, wet clothes, and everything else that she felt she would never care to eat again. Only God sustained her, and he seemed far, far away: she was more likely to go to him than to find him coming to her.

It was the promise of a new day when Professor Stowe, deserting Lyman's Lane, received an appointment (1850) to the faculty of his alma mater, Bowdoin College at Brunswick, Maine.

Forty Years of Subservience

And what, the reader may ask, through all these early years, may be said of Harriet herself? Except for her writing, the main story of her first forty years is the record of what she bore from others.

This repressed life was eventually, of course, not as unproductive as it seemed. Without her family exactly as it was, she could never have written her books exactly as she did. Catherine's life was essential for *The Minister's Wooing,* Calvin Stowe's for *Oldtown Folks.* From her early sketch "Uncle Tim" to her last book, *Poganuc People,* forty-odd years later, Lyman Beecher's character, life, and ancestry furnished details without which she could not have worked; and over this same period of time the dead mother, Roxana, and her own dead infant son furnished equally essential dreams. For her material, Stowe was more indebted to her family than most novelists have been.

On a less objective level, these early repressions were no less significant: when she ceased being imprisoned in the strange country of the West, her smoldering nature expanded into full expression. Before 1850, however, she had attempted no estimate of herself except as an individual. She had witnessed exciting public events without participating in them; antiabolitionist riots in the streets of Cincinnati and proabolitionist rebellion at Lane Seminary took place outside the accepted field of a woman's interest. She had not broken discipline by becoming a suffragist or propagandist for any public cause. Her private duties as obedient daughter and wife had demanded almost more energy than she had to give, and she had taken refuge from overwork in the consolation of heavenly love: to mistrust the world, to accept it as the abode of cruelty and injustice, was the philosophy by which she lived.

Once the foreign environment of Cincinnati was thrown off, she began to feel better. Every stage of the journey that carried her toward New England lightened her burdens by taking her farther from at least two members of her family, and one can see how, with the release of this pressure and the improvement of health that accompanied it, the frustrated woman might throw herself into a work of self-expression. For more reasons than one, then, Professor Stowe's appointment to the faculty of Bowdoin College held a world of promise for his wife as well as for him. This promise, though genuine, was slow of fulfillment, and in the periods immediately preceding and during the writing of *Uncle Tom's Cabin,* her mind was still turbulent and restless.

Completing the story was almost impossibly difficult. She was entering a new world of national politics yet was still an overworked housewife harassed by personal frustrations, debts, and family difficulties. Consequently, the unexpected, amazing popularity of *Uncle Tom's Cabin,* when it came, revolutionized her life, bringing freedom, celebrity, prestige, and prosperity.

Chapter Two
Early Writings

The Mayflower (1843)

Authorship was as much a fact of life for the Beechers as churchgoing. The family lived on words, spoken and written. The father's table talk was as lively as his sermons, many of which were printed and distributed nationally. Catherine became a prolific writer, as did Henry Ward. Edward and Charles also produced books. Harriet fitted the family pattern, with the important exception that the kind of literary work she undertook was brief fiction for commercial magazines. This became her apprenticeship, her part-time employment from 1833 until her venture into the larger form of the serial story.

These early sketches deserve attention for several reasons. Negligible as they seem, they earned her a place among writers for the minor magazines of the period. As a body they clearly show the direction of her talent and the public for which she wrote. Some were reprinted in her first book, *The Mayflower* (1843), others in an enlarged edition of the same work, following the success of *Uncle Tom's Cabin,* but the majority were never collected.

The small volume called *The Mayflower* was as modest as its subtitle suggested: "Sketches of Scenes and Characters among the Descendants of the Puritans." The stories themselves, typical of the domestic fiction of the time, exhibit neither the strength nor the originality to suggest the later success and fame of their author. From the very first sketch the reader must be resigned to the familiar looseness in plot and characterization of the household fiction of the gift annuals and the ladies magazines.

"Love *versus* Law," as this longish tale is called, is built in the casual way popular before Poe (in *Tales of the Grotesque and Arabesque* [1840]) and Hawthorne (in *Twice-Told Tales* [1837]) had introduced conscious unity of effect. Starting with some gentle reflections on Christian old age, "Love *versus* Law" progresses to a characterization of Deacon Enos Dudley, who is contrasted with his fellow officer, Deacon Abrams.

When interest has been aroused in these two gentlemen, they are both dropped from the story—Deacon Abrams permanently—while the action moves into the bosom of the Jones family. Two orphaned "girls," to use the author's word, the elder, Silence, verging on forty and the younger just eighteen, introduce a new complication; for their dead father has cheated Deacon Enos out of five hundred dollars, and the only way he can collect is by taking the money from the legacy of the younger girl, the beautiful and tender Susan. Understandably enough, he hesitates.

Stowe's story is not yet quite begun, for another family is needed to save Susan from unhappy poverty. Uncle Jaw Adams, a crabbed and contentious New Englander, has long been at odds with his neighbors, suing or threatening to sue them for innumerable grievances, fancied or real. At the moment, his heart is set on collecting damages from the Jones girls, because their father and he had never agreed on the exact boundaries between their farms. Solely for the reader's benefit, the whole story of the Jones-Adams feud is poured into good Deacon Enos's unwilling ears. When all the familiar details have tumbled out in a torrent of colloquialisms, the author pauses to announce, "But all this while the deacon had been in a profound meditation concerning the ways and means of putting a stop to a quarrel that had been his torment from time immemorial, and just at this moment a plan had struck his mind which our story will proceed to unfold."[1]

This promise of action is further delayed to introduce one other key character, the son of old Uncle Jaw. Young Joseph Adams has been away at college, and the Deacon's plan is the simple one of inducing the boy to marry Susan Jones, thus settling the feud between the families without recourse to the ugly "law" of the title. In the spirit of "love" he plans to contribute to the young folks his five-hundred-dollar claim against the Jones estate.

From this point the complications diminish, and the match between the young people proceeds without genuine obstacle. Of course the stern and inconsiderate older sister fails to realize the meaning of love to a delicate young girl; and of course the hard-hearted father forbids his son to court the daughter of a traditional enemy. Against the basic goodness of human nature these demonstrations mean nothing. All such people are fundamentally good, Stowe shows, once their better natures are appealed to, and love is bound to win. Thus this New England Romeo and Juliet, on a suitably modest scale, reach the happy ending of consummated love. The final paragraph of the tale is significant enough to quote.

And, accordingly, many happy years flew over the heads of the young couple in the Stanton place, long after the hoary hairs of their kind benefactor, the deacon, were laid with reverence in the dust. Uncle Jaw was so far wrought upon by the magnanimity of the good old man as to be very materially changed for the better. Instead of quarreling in real earnest all around the neighborhood, he confined himself merely to battling the opposite side of every question with his son; which, as the latter was somewhat of a logician, afforded a pretty good field for the exercise of his powers; and he was heard to declare, at the funeral of the old deacon, that "after all, a man got as much, and maybe more, to go along as the deacon did, than to be all the time fisting and jawing"; "though I tell you what it is," said he, afterward, " 'taint every one that has the deacon's *faculty,* anyhow."[2]

The connections between this tale and Stowe's life are obvious. Silence Jones is not exactly Catherine Beecher, yet her relationship with her younger sister is similar to Catherine's with Harriet. The contentious Uncle Jaw is not Lyman Beecher, but the relationship between him and his son is precisely that of the elder and younger Beechers. Young Joseph Adams is not Henry Ward Beecher; yet Susan's pride of him, especially as valedictorian, is precisely that which Harriet took in her favorite brother. "If ever a woman feels proud of her lover," she was to write in *Dred* years later, "it is when she sees him as a successful speaker."[3]

In addition to such personal details, the story owes to Stowe's past its whole New England setting, which is its best feature. The place has atmosphere, the characters belong, their actions and reactions are appropriate. There are elements of realism and local color, especially in touches of dialect. This last was no novelty in 1843, since well before this date two New England ladies had established themselves, through magazine sketches and complete novels, as local colorists of note. The names of Catherine M. Sedgwick[4] and Lydia H. Sigourney, now almost forgotten, were among the brightest. The latter especially, contributing to over three hundred different magazines, was both the Edna St. Vincent Millay and the Kathleen Norris of her age.

In Sigourney's little-studied *Sketch of Connecticut, Forty Years Since,* published in 1824, a true forerunner of Stowe's work is found. Although there is much of the literary lady about Sigourney—with her elegant manners and her chapter epigrams from Goldsmith, Warton, and other proper poets—her book hits most of the topics Stowe later developed. Like Stowe, she enjoyed references to Saturday night baked beans and other such local customs; and, like her, she also breathed the full spirit of love for the land. Writing of Connecticut, Sigourney said, precisely as Stowe would have, "There, was exhibited the singular example of an aristocracy, less intent upon family aggrandizement, than upon becoming illustrious in virtue."[5]

Dialect abounds in the *Sketch of Connecticut,* but it is restricted, as in "Love *versus* Law," to the humble characters, and especially to a certain Farmer Larkin. "Your ha-ath too, is as clean as a cheeny tea-cup, Ma'am. I hate to put my coarse huffs on it. But I ha'nt been used to seein' kiverlids spread on the floor to walk on. We are glad to get 'em to kiver us up with a nights. This looks like a boughten one. . . . Tis exceedin' curous."[6]

There is a full store of such talk, for Sigourney's Farmer Larkin is as garrulous a man as Sam Lawson of Stowe's later *Oldtown Folks* and *Sam Lawson's Oldtown Fireside Stories.* "But Tim, the third child, he's the boy for larnin'. He took a prodigous likin' to books, when he was a baby; and if you only show'd him one, he's put it rite into his mouth, and stop squallin'. He 'ant but eleven year old now; and when he gets a newspaper, there's no *whoa* to him, no more than to our black ox when he sees the haystack, till he's read it clear through, advertisements and all."[7] This is truly the New England manner as Stowe also understood it.

The Mayflower volume of 1843 contained fifteen sketches, several of which would repay as careful study as "Love *versus* Law." In brief, *The Mayflower* foreshadows much of Stowe's later writing. "Trials of a Housekeeper" was the first of many reactions to the servant problem. "Let Every Man Mind His Own Business" was her first contribution to the temperance crusade for which, following her father's lead, she was always ready to say a kindly word. Her impulse for reform showed in her advocacy of special Sunday services for children ("The Sabbath"), kinder treatment of tradespeople ("The Seamstress"), and greater financial support for religious institutions ("So Many Calls"). The first of her long series of pathetic death scenes were found in "Uncle Tim" and in "Little Edward," in which the demise of a perfect child was recounted.

In addition to these themes, which she would develop later, the half-dozen New England sketches in the book, the only ones that justified the subtitle, thinly covered ground that she was subsequently to cultivate thoroughly. "Old Father Morris," the best designed of the series, presented an old-fashioned type of preacher. "Cousin William," planned along the same lines as "Love *versus* Law," introduced in Mrs. Abigail Evetts a busybody or reformer gone wrong. "The Sabbath" contained in its opening section a moving description of church services in the old days.

"Uncle Tim," another in this New England series, was not only the most famous of the group—it was a prize winner—but was highly enough esteemed to be reprinted in 1834, soon after its appearance in James Hall's *Western Monthly Magazine*. "Uncle Tim" appeared as *A New England Sketch*, a booklet of fifty-two pages, with publisher Mr. Gilman's notice on the reverse of the title page. "The following story was introduced to the public through the *Western Monthly Magazine*, a popular periodical; and the publisher's only object in throwing it before the community in this form, is that an effort so successful to delineate the character of New Englanders, by one of their daughters, may be preserved."[8]

"Throwing it before the community," an inept phrase with which to introduce a new writer's effort, is a marvel of elegant flattery in comparison with Catherine Beecher's well-meant but patronizing comments in her preface to *The Mayflower*. Without conscious malice, the elder sister was only following her bent, for she had admired Harriet's writing sufficiently to allow some of it to be published as her own. She would not try to praise her sister's sketches, Catherine said, describing them coldly as "written by a young mother and housekeeper in the first years of her novitiate." She confessed her own interest as editor to be solely a general one in moral fiction as a type of writing preferable to the frivolous stories of Dickens, and she offered *The Mayflower* as an example of what might be attempted, without vouching for Harriet's "qualifications" for doing the work well.

The Mayflower was no sensation. Harper and Brothers discontinued it within a few years, and it was forgotten until after the success of *Uncle Tom's Cabin*, when it was republished (a single sketch, "So Many Calls," was dropped) as part of a much larger collection of articles and stories called *The May Flower, and Miscellaneous Writings* (1855). The twenty-one new sketches were in general similar to the original fifteen. Two more temperance tales appeared besides "Let Every Man Mind His Own Business," strengthening Stowe's position as a consistent prohibitionist rather than as one who merely favored prohibition. A few poems were also added, but the only contribution showing a new thematic interest was "The Two Altars"—written in 1851—a strong attack on Negro slavery, a subject that had meant so little to Stowe in 1843 that no allusion to it can be found in the entire original *Mayflower*.

The lukewarm reception of her first collection of stories did not perturb Stowe as much as might be expected, for she regarded book publication as a sideline. The compilation had in all probability been, as Catherine hinted in the preface, not Harriet's idea, but Catherine's. Their joint textbook, a school geography published in 1833, had likewise been Catherine's plan, for she was the educator in the family and the senior collaborator on the book. Thus when *The Mayflower* led to no permanent alliance with the publishing firm of Harper and Brothers, Harriet shed no tears and uttered no lamentations.

In truth, at this time her ambitions were still held at the level of periodical publication. Books were a distant world, beyond her reach, whereas magazines were as near as her fellow members of Cincinnati's literary Semi-Colon Club. She knew personally editors James Hall of the *Western Monthly Magazine* and E. D. Mansfield of the Cincinnati *Chronicle*. Other periodicals were almost as easily reached, and they paid two dollars a page for sketches that she could turn out between her housekeeping chores. In comparison with this assured income, small as it was, the financial returns from books were more than doubtful. Even *Uncle Tom's Cabin*, her first longer work, was originally written for a periodical. Intended as a few short sketches, it grew into two volumes, but subsequent book publication was looked upon merely as a problematic addition to the original three hundred dollars received from the *National Era*.

The effect of this attitude toward writing can be seen in Stowe's work from the beginning to the end of her career. Even in her later years, when her books sold well, they were first published in magazines—with *Dred* and *Oldtown Folks* the only significant exceptions. She wrote, that is, from month to month, or usually from week to week, a cruel schedule that promoted rapid composition and prevented systematic revision.

For an understanding of her writings, early or late, a glance at the magazines that accepted her work is essential. The logical place to begin is the *Western Monthly Magazine*, her first market.

Contributions to Cincinnati Publications

When the Beechers reached Cincinnati in October 1832, the city's literary colony was agog over the promised new periodical, the *Western Monthly Magazine*, to be started the following January. Actually the

Western Monthly was not entirely new, for it was a continuation of the *Illinois Monthly Magazine,* which had been issued since October 1830. Nevertheless, the establishment of a high-class literary journal in Cincinnati was the cause of justifiable excitement.

No less enticing was the character of the editor, Judge James Hall, whom Harriet Beecher soon met. Hall had been soldier, lawyer, and politician, as well as jurist, writer, and editor. His manner was dynamic, and his literary work was dominated by consciously held theories, which he expressed repeatedly with clarity and persuasiveness, and which Harriet Beecher soon adopted. As his literary platform Hall advocated cheerfulness, morality, and regionalism. He was an outstanding defender of fiction, and with rollicking good humor that sometimes became biting satire he opened endless vistas of promise for young writers of the West.

Hall was also, as his references to the fair sex clearly show, a chivalrous admirer of women writers. By accepting their work for his magazines he proved how highly he esteemed what he called "those attractive attributes of the female pen, and of the female heart, pure morality and delicate sentiment."[9] All of these attitudes were to be carried over from the *Illinois Monthly* to the *Western Monthly,* the only difference being that under its new name the publication was expected to be, as indeed it was, bigger and better.

Harriet Beecher, newly arrived from New England, could hardly have immediately known that to become a contributor to the new magazine she would need to exhibit in her writing cheerful energy, local color, and refined morality. She could not have remained long in ignorance, for Hall was his own press agent. In the January 1833 issue, the opening note, "To the Reader," would have been especially interesting to the prospective contributor. "We live in a country and an age, governed by moral influence," was a proposition to which the youngest Miss Beecher would murmur a hearty assent. "The literature of our country has never exerted the influence to which it is entitled," was another to set one thinking. How was the *Western Monthly* to meet this problem? The editor, who made a special appeal to educators, explained, "Although devoted chiefly to elegant literature, it has always been our wish and endeavor, to render it useful, by making it the medium of disseminating valuable information and pure moral principles."[10] Without this definite endorsement of virtue, Hall might never have enlisted the interest of the Beechers. He had appealed, that is, to their dominant concern.

Satisfactory as his opening note was, Hall followed it with an even more significant and suggestive article entitled "American Literature." The emphasis was partly patriotic but mainly financial. Stowe's later professional attitude toward her writing—namely, to get all she could from it—was encouraged, if not actually instigated, by Hall. The English people, he pointed out, paid their writers much more generously than Americans did, and he complained especially that native book publishers rejected native works because they objected to paying authors' royalties. "The American writer must give his labor for nothing," he protested, "or be driven from the field by this disadvantageous competition." To improve the condition of American writers, he urged greater financial support for American periodicals. "Patronage should *come first,*" he insisted; then literary journals could afford to pay their writers better. [11]

Harriet must have sat down immediately to do some writing, for her first contribution, "Modern Uses of Language," appeared in the third issue. Signed simply "B," it was attributed to Catherine Beecher, though it was Harriet's work (CES, 69). While the elder sister took public credit, the younger found what was more important and valuable: an introduction to the art of pleasing editors.

Not much need be said about this light essay. In it Harriet maintained whimsically that the modern uses of language are to conceal either ideas or the lack of them. She drew her examples of obscurity from Milton and Dugald Stewart and her examples of empty clichés from undesignated minor writers. Her motto, chosen with inevitable cleverness, was Hamlet's "Words, words, words!"

The next high spot in the *Western Monthly* is to be found in the sixth issue, June 1833. A brief review, much the briefest for the month, it can be quoted here completely.

Primary Geography for Children, on an improved plan, with twelve maps, and numerous engravings. By C. and H. Beecher, Principals of the Western Female Institute. Cincinnati: Corey and Fairbank.

This is a very capital little book. The authoresses are accomplished young ladies, who have made the tuition of youth their study and business for several years, and who unite to a competent knowledge of the subject, an intimate acquaintance with the best modes of teaching children. Writing books for children is one of the most difficult, and surely one of the most useful branches of authorship. We most cordially recommend this, as a successful effort in this noble field. [12]

The issue of September 1833 offered A PREMIUM OF FIFTY DOLLARS—all in capital letters—for a story and a similar prize for an essay. In December the essay appeared as scheduled, "Themes for Western Fiction," by Isaac Appleton Jewett. Since it gave Hall his own ideas back again, he commended it highly. At the same time, he extended the story contest, since no worthy entries had been received. When a decision was finally reached, the winning story, by Harriet Beecher, was used to open the issue of April 1834. While the award for the short story contest was being held back, Harriet's story "Isabelle and Her Sister Kate and Their Cousin" appeared in the February 1834 issue of the magazine.[13] This story, signed "May," preceded by two months the prize-winning "New England Sketch" that had usually been considered her first published story. Nor can there be any doubt of the authorship, as the following abstract will show.

Miss Isabelle is very beautiful and popular; her young sister Kate is plain but nice. She excels in "being happy," in spite of her social eclipse. "She had a world of sprightliness, a deal of simplicity and affection, with a dash of goodnatured shrewdness," and she adored her elder sister. The girls are visited by their cousin Edward, a valedictorian. The whole town gossips about his affection for the grand Isabelle, but he is really in love with quiet, retiring Kate. "No, Miss Catherine, it's you!" he finally blurts out. The last paragraph reads: "Poor little Kate! it was her turn to look at the cotton balls, and to exhibit symptoms of scarlet fever; and while she is thinking what to say next, you may read the next piece in the magazine."

The similarity of these situations to later stories by Stowe— especially "Love *versus* Law"—does not need to be pointed out. The sketch was also reprinted five years later, under Harriet's name, in the Cincinnati *Chronicle,* though never in any of her books.

Following the prize story in April, Hall used her "Frankness" in May, attributing it to "A Lady," and in July, "Sister Mary," with her initials. These three, reprinted in *The Mayflower* of 1843, show to what extent the young writer was developing a recognizable and commercially valuable theme and manner of her own. The part played by James Hall in developing this manner deserves specific mention. For a short time he was to her what Lowell became after the founding of the *Atlantic:* a restraining influence on sentimentality, and an encouragement to her better qualities of observation and humor.[14]

Of much less importance than the *Western Monthly Magazine,* but still essential to an appreciation of Stowe's early literary activities, is her relationship to two Cincinnati weekly papers, the *Chronicle* and the *Journal*. The case for the *Chronicle* is stated by its one-time editor, E. D. Mansfield. "Mrs. Stowe, then Miss Beecher, published her first stories in it."[15] The explanation of this error is that these "first stories" were *reprinted* in the *Chronicle,* and that Mansfield, after forty-five years, did not remember quite correctly.

At various dates beginning 3 May 1834, the *Chronicle* reprinted Harriet's stories. The prize tale, the first to be so honored, took the whole of page one and half of page two; it was perhaps the longest contribution ever to appear in a single issue of the *Chronicle*. "It is a beauteous tale," wrote the editor, "and bears the stamp of genius." Later in the same month the *Chronicle* reprinted "Frankness" without the author's name. Four years later, under Mansfield's editorship, "Frankness" was again reprinted, to be followed by "Cousin William" and "Isabelle and Her Sister Kate and Their Cousin." After it had grown into a daily, the *Chronicle* continued the policy of reprinting Stowe's tales.

Her connection with the *Journal and Western Luminary* was closer, though here again the literary importance of the connection was slight. The *Journal*, a weekly Presbyterian paper, was deeply devoted to Lyman Beecher and Lane Seminary; and it was also on close terms with the New York *Evangelist,* one of Stowe's other markets. While the *Journal*'s editor, T. Brainerd, was out of town at the general assembly of his church, his place was taken by young Henry Ward Beecher as editor pro tem. The year was 1836, and as Professor Stowe was also away on a mission to investigate European education, his young wife was free to assist her brother with the *Journal.* How much she assisted him is a question, since her writing for the paper was without byline and not personal enough to reveal her authorship. The experience put her inside a publisher's office, initiating her into the mechanical and commercial aspects of publication, an abiding interest.

Contributions to Eastern Publications

From the Cincinnati *Journal* to the New York *Evangelist* was a greater step geographically than culturally, for both were staunchly Presbyterian. The *Evangelist* accurately described itself as "Devoted to Revivals, Doctrinal Discussion and Religious Intelligence Generally." It reprinted matter from the Cincinnati *Journal,* thereby repaying the *Journal*'s compliment in kind. The medium of Harriet Beecher's introduction to the *Evangelist* is thus easily seen: she was led to it by her family, rather than introduced by a literary outsider like James Hall.

The *Evangelist* also ran a department of "Secular Intelligence" and used nonsectarian material of a moralizing tendency by writers like Sigourney. Harriet's first contribution (1835), initialed "E. B.," was a temperance tale entitled "Uncle Enoch," a plotless but not pointless narrative of how a benevolent deacon induces people to sign the abstainer's pledge. To add that the kind deacon has three lovely daughters who help in his work is to complete the story.

Sixteen years later, in 1851, almost on the verge of *Uncle Tom's Cabin*, Stowe was still writing for the *Evangelist*. During the intervening years her offerings had been neither frequent nor significant, but some were reprinted in her collections of 1843 and 1855. Of the unreprinted pieces several deal with the need of giving money to religious causes. One speaks of the possibility of spiritualism, a subject of great interest to her later. Others present, mildly but firmly, her family's objections to the Roman Catholics. In addition to these strictly religious papers, a few had wider appeal, like two articles on "Literary Epidemics."

Meanwhile, as if in emulation of Sigourney—who stopped counting after she had published two thousand pieces in periodicals—Stowe was releasing her work through a surprisingly large number of magazines and gift annuals. Sigourney's own *Religious Souvenir* opened its pages to her. So did the *Christian Keepsake*, which numbered among its contributors Sigourney, Sarah Josepha Hale, and Catherine Beecher. *The Gift*, as has been mentioned, printed "Love *versus* Law" under the editorship of Miss Leslie, and somebody was so struck by another of Stowe's tales, "Mark Meridan," that it was published as part of a book, in company with a story by Miss Leslie herself and two by T. S. Arthur.[16] The august *Token*, the aristocrat of the annuals, printed one of her most characteristic early stories, "The Yankee Girl," which was not reprinted until 1972 but is interesting because it foreshadows—in the clash between a sturdy New England maiden and a questionable aristocrat— a situation used in *The Minister's Wooing* and in *Oldtown Folks*.[17] Her work also appeared in the *Banquet*, the *Christian Souvenir*, and the *Violet*, as well as, later, in T. S. Arthur's *Temperance Offering* for 1853. The complete list of her contributions to the annuals shows industrious marketing as well as industrious writing.

Godey's Lady's Book, another of her regular markets, made much the same appeal as many of the annuals. Though it published work by some important authors—Emerson, Poe, Irving—its mainstays were such tried and true minor figures as Sigourney, who was also a member of the editorial board; Frances Osgood; Caroline Hentz of Cincinnati; Miss Leslie; M. St. Leon Loud; Hannah Gould; and T. S. Arthur. Among Stowe's efforts never reclaimed from this publication are a moral tale about a spoiled girl and poor housekeeper, "The Only Daughter"; a skit, "Olympiana," in which Greek deities were modernized in the style of 1840; and a secular poem translated from Goethe.

A complete analysis of Stowe's commercial writing preceding *Uncle Tom's Cabin* would be more wearisome than profitable. Some complaisant editors were not concerned with verbal niceties, but she could write as carefully as the more exacting ones demanded. "The Yankee Girl" is as superior to "The Seamstress" as the *Token* is to the *Religious Souvenir*. As the best of these sketches show, she had learned a valuable lesson: to be freshly observant and moral, with flashes of Yankee wit and frontier humor.

This salutary principle was, however, in conflict with another that might be attributed to the *Evangelist* or, further back, to sister Catherine's pedagogy: the desire to do good sometimes refused to be kept within intelligent limits. The annuals allowed her to run wild, confirming her habit of easy, conventional writing without challenging her keenness of expression or thought. "The Tea-Rose," a special favorite of Mrs. Hale's, is only one example of many aesthetic misfortunes.[18]

Young Stowe's Type of Writer

Now that the details have been set down, let us consider the picture they make. Just how far did all this writing take young Stowe, and where did it leave her? Isn't there a long jump between these trifles and *Uncle Tom's Cabin?* To answer the first of these questions—for the jump to *Uncle Tom's Cabin* is not so amazing as Eliza's jump across the Ohio River—this early writing gave Stowe membership in a distinct group of women writers of the time, with whom she never ceased to have a relationship. Like other women writers, she was required by custom to be definitely identified as married or unmarried. To be unmarried like Catherine Beecher was no disgrace, more likely a misfortune; but "Mrs." was a title of great respect, more prestigious than "Miss," and in many settings practically a part of the lucky female's name. In private life Harriet would not have recognized her name without the "Mrs.":

Stowe meant Calvin, whose helpmeet she was. In the household magazines she was likewise the wife.

When Harriet Beecher decided to write professionally she had three distinct possibilities to explore. The heady intellectual woman of today was represented only by Margaret Fuller; and the independent experimenter, like Emily Dickinson or Gertrude Stein, was far in the future. Lacking these, the early nineteenth century offered only the three types—the sublimely epic, the passionately romantic, and the piously domestic. [19] Harriet specialized almost entirely in the third.

Among women writers on the grand scale, the most outstanding was Maria Gowen Brooks, known as Maria del Occidente, whose biblical epic *Zophiël* was lavishly praised by Rufus Griswold, Robert Southey, and Charles Lamb. Amid her rich rhymes and battery of poetic names like Egla and Meles, Brooks's admiring contemporaries found beauties equal to Dante and Milton. Louisa J. Hall, another of the type admiringly represented in Griswold's *Female Poets of America,* was noted for her *Miriam,* a poetic drama of early Christianity.

On such sublimity Stowe sternly, if perhaps reluctantly, turned her back. Her childhood tragedy of *Cleon,* which introduced the cruelties of Nero, had been indeed just such a play as Hall's *Miriam* or Elizabeth Oakes-Smith's *The Roman Tribute;* and the record states that she abandoned it with sadness. In her professional days, though many magazines welcomed such flights into baseless grandeur, she was seldom tempted. A sketch in *The May Flower* of 1855, a description of Christ's procession to the cross, is one of her few attempts in this vein. An epic vision from the *Evangelist,* "Now we see through a glass darkly," was never salvaged. There are passages in her novels, however, that recall the "grace and godlike majesty" of Hall's; in fact, her Italian novel, *Agnes of Sorrento,* was planned too nearly in the same vein for its own good.

As romantic passion meant so much less to her than sublimity, Stowe was less tempted by the lures of feminine eroticism. Critics and magazine editors might be susceptible to melodious lovelorn maidens, but not Calvin Stowe's wife. In Byron and de Staël she had encountered wayward sentiments, but she kept them, when she could, for such misled, pathetic creatures as the light-headed girls in *The Pearl of Orr's Island* and in *Pink and White Tyranny.* From the beginning she shunned girlish love-longing for the soberer sentiments of the Christian wife and mother.

Though not the only temperament among early nineteenth-century literary women, this last was by far the most popular. Sigourney and Sedgwick were no more perfect in their pious resignation than Hannah Gould, the housekeeper poetess, a steady contributor to the *Western Monthly*. But the ones most worthy of observation, as showing on a large scale the fine flower of the tradition in which Stowe worked, were the young women: Susan Warner, author of *The Wide, Wide World,* the great success of 1850; and Elizabeth Prentiss, author of *Stepping Heavenward,* a lesser success of 1869. Warner prepared the way for Stowe's success, and Prentiss, entirely without literary encouragement, carried religious emotionalism to its ultimate extreme.

As far as *The Wide, Wide World* is concerned, its account is easily reckoned; for pathos and piety were the leading ingredients of this lengthy account of a troubled girlhood. Sent from New York City into the country by her dying mother, Ellen Montgomery suffers under a harsh but not inhuman paternal aunt; finds godly friends; and, after becoming an orphan, repeats the round of suffering and friendship under the affectionate but rough guardianship of a maternal uncle. A sweet and studious girl, she grows sweeter and more studious through adversity, finally becoming a true Christian on Stowe's own model, earnest and charitable, strict with herself but tender toward others.[20]

Stepping Heavenward, which was published in book form in 1869 after serialization in a church paper, is an almost classic distillation of nineteenth-century sentimental piety.[21] In form, the book is the journal of Katherine Mortimer; beginning in 1831, when the girl is sixteen years old, it relates her growth into grace, as marriage and suffering transform the rebellious imp of nature into a saintly mother. The reader's last glimpse of her is as a bedridden invalid. The old family physician is visiting her.

"Ah, these lovely children are explained now," he said.
"Do you really think," I asked "that it has been good for my children to have a feeble, afflicted mother?"
"Yes, I really think so. A disciplined mother—disciplined children."
This comforting thought is one of the last drops in a cup of felicity already full.[22]

To this extreme of self-abnegation Harriet Beecher Stowe might have come had not the Congress of the United States enacted a law so repulsive that she consciously rebelled against it. The Fugitive Slave Act of 1850 outraged her as it outraged millions, and raised her passive opposition to slavery to a passionate resolution to bring about its end. As she wrote the weekly chapters of *Uncle Tom's Cabin,* freedom for the black slaves of the South was in the forefront of her mind; but the theme broadened until it became universal: freedom for the blacks, freedom for herself, freedom for all women, freedom for the lowly everywhere, freedom for all of God's creatures.

Chapter Three
Uncle Tom's Cabin

Designs

Only a child can read *Uncle Tom's Cabin* without preconceptions. William Dean Howells, aged fourteen, read it under ideal conditions, week by week, as a serial story by an unknown author. Each chapter was fresh, the picture was clear, the reader could not know what would come next or how the story would end. Above all, the original *Uncle Tom's Cabin* serial was a story, not a controversy. It induced its readers—a special interest group—to weep a lot, laugh a little, become indignant, and perhaps even resolve to lead a better life. As a brand new book, however, offered to the nation and the world, it reached a hostile as well as a sympathetic audience, becoming at once a document with political implications. Over the years it has been the most discussed book in American history, and by now no person who reads it or, certainly, writes about it can see it with the fresh approach of Howells and other enthusiastic readers of the *National Era*. Every synopsis is an analysis, every chapter a question.

What is *Uncle Tom's Cabin* about? To the original readers is was about slavery in the South, a story about weak and wicked people, strong and virtuous people, from fiends to saints. It pleaded for the end of slavery, with the narrator often speaking to the reader, making herself a character in the story. With emancipation accomplished and the original purpose attained (though not in the way Stowe had intended or foreseen) new readers have discovered other themes of enduring importance: family life, racial differences, the superiority of women, personal and social redemption. The meaning of *Uncle Tom's Cabin* has become as debated as its factual accuracy was contested when Stowe wrote it as a description of the life of its time.

Yet the book is a story, no matter how many messages it carries, and the substance could be compressed into a paragraph for some technical purposes, the design is so easily stated. It is one of the Victorian novels in which, according to a common practice, the adventures of two groups of characters are alternated to give an inclusive picture of society and to provide a variety of emotional appeal.

In *Uncle Tom's Cabin* the contrasting groups begin as slaves in the border state of Kentucky. Tom, an intelligent black man in early middle age, is sold southward down the river. His experiences, forming the main plot, introduce numerous types of slaveholders and their human possessions. In the second plot Eliza, a young yellow-skinned matron and one of Tom's fellow slaves, is the central figure. As she, her child, and her husband flee to Canada various characters are introduced who are typical of the abolitionist enthusiasts along the Underground Railway.

For the greater part, the two distinct plots are developed with an almost architectural balance, extending to the obvious strong contrast between the final refuge of Eliza's party in free Ontario and the last solitary misery of Tom in despotic Louisiana. This main design is easily kept in mind, and for a clear conception of the story as story one need add only a few other characters, without many more details than might appear as notes along with the dramatis personae of a printed play.

In approximate order of their appearance the reader meets:

Mr. Shelby, Tom's first owner, a Kentucky gentleman forced by economic stringency to sell Tom in spite of the humanitarian objections of Mrs. Shelby and the affection of Master Shelby.

Haley, a crude slave dealer who buys both Tom and Eliza's little boy, for resale; his friend Loker, a more brutal slave dealer than Haley.

Slaves on the Shelby plantation, including Tom's wife, Chloe, and Sam, a clever rascal.

George Harris, Eliza's husband, a talented, nearly white slave on a neighboring plantation, who also escapes to Canada and eventual reunion with his wife and child.

Workers on the Underground Railway: specifically, Mrs. Bird and her husband, a state senator in Ohio; various Quakers; and others necessary to the action but not carried throughout the story.

Mr. Augustine St. Clare, Tom's second kind owner, prevented by sudden death from freeing Tom; his sister from Vermont, Miss Ophelia, the voice of righteousness according to old Calvinistic standards; his wife, Marie, a cruel and vain southern aristocrat; their saintly daughter Eva.

Slaves in the St. Clare household, notably Topsy, an undisciplined youngster about the age of Eva.

Simon Legree, Tom's third owner, viciousness incarnate, defiler of
women, torturer of the helpless, and murderer of Tom.
Slaves on Legree's plantation, pathetic female victims of his lust, and
malicious or sodden male representations of the worst that slavery
can do.

Although the skeleton of the story is now before the reader, the
substance of the book eludes such tabulation, for the power and indi-
viduality of *Uncle Tom's Cabin* consist less in this conventional literary
material from the public domain than in the special vitality infused
into it. The missionary spirit in which she began, hoping to persuade
owners to free their slaves voluntarily, diminished and expired as she
viewed her subject with less sentimental optimism and more horror. "I
write with my heart's blood," her son quotes; "I suffer exquisitely in
writing these things." Suffering with Eliza and Tom, "many times . . .
I thought my health would fail utterly" (CES 198, 203). When she
finished with the scenes of Tom's martyrdom the plea for reform that
had been her original plan had been transformed into a stern demand.[1]

The Opening Chapters

To turn to the opening pages of *Uncle Tom's Cabin* is to be introduced
to a lady with an acute sense of propriety. "For convenience' sake, we
have said, hitherto, two *gentlemen*. One of the parties, however, when
critically examined, did not seem strictly speaking to come under the
species." Continuing with the description of the questionable party
drinking wine in a well-furnished dining parlor in a Kentucky town,
one soon suspects the author of a distaste for the fellow. He was
overdressed, she complains, wore too much jewelry, spoke ungrammati-
cally, and indulged in "various profane expressions, which not even the
desire to be graphic in our account shall induce us to transcribe."
As the objectionable Haley sits talking with Mr. Shelby, drinking
his reluctant host's wine and brandy, the narrative proper is promptly
begun by the mention of Tom, not yet avuncular, whose virtues are
extolled by the master to the prospective purchaser. Eliza's child, rushing into the room and performing an impromptu minstrel act with
singing, dancing, and mimicking, is soon followed by his mother, a
quadroon of about twenty-five whose ravishing beauty draws justified
praise from the businesslike slave dealer. With economy and skill—the
author was never to do as neat an opening again—the drama has already

started, for the dismayed mother, Eliza, has recognized the slave trader's mission. The terror that is one of the dominant notes of the book is clearly indicated in an impassioned interview between her and her mistress.

Meanwhile the crass Haley has expressed what Stowe consistently regarded as the most dangerous heresy about the Negroes. "These critters ain't like white folks, you know," he explains, a denial of humanity to the slaves that was anathema to Stowe.

Throughout the first chapter Stowe forces Haley to damn himself through his own speeches, only to weaken the effect by permitting Mr. Shelby to damn him in soliloquy. In the art of fiction, it soon becomes apparent, Stowe has not left behind her *Lady's Book* mannerisms.

In the second chapter, Eliza and her husband become the center of attention. The young black man, to whom is ascribed mechanical genius equal to Eli Whitney's, is shown as the victim of an envious master's hatred. "Yes, Eliza, it's all misery, misery, misery! My life is bitter as wormwood; the very life is burning out of me. I'm a poor, miserable, forlorn drudge. . . . My master! and who made him my master? That's what I think of,—what right has he to me? I'm a man as much as he is. I'm a better man than he is. I know more about business than he does" (*UTC,* 18, chap 2).

In spite of this emphatic preparation, the foreshadowed escape is transferred to Eliza. The spectacular climax, Eliza's wild leap out of her pursuers' clutches and across the Ohio River, is well known— somewhat inaccurately, for there were no bloodhounds on the shore in the original, only in Aiken's play. In Stowe's words:

She caught her child and sprang down the steps. . . . In that dizzy moment her feet to her scarce seemed to touch the ground, and a moment brought her to the water's edge. Right on behind they came; and, nerved with strength such as God gives only to the desperate, with one wild cry and flying leap, she vaulted sheer over the turbid current by the shore, on to the rafter of ice beyond. It was a desperate leap,—impossible to anything but madness and despair. . . . The huge green fragment of ice on which she alighted pitched and creaked as her weight came on it, but she stayed there not a moment. With wild cries and desperate energy she leaped to another and still another cake; stumbling,—leaping,—slipping,—springing upwards again! Her shoes were gone,—her stockings cut from her feet,—while blood marked every step; but she saw nothing, felt nothing, till dimly, as in a dream, she saw the Ohio side, and a man helping her up the bank. (*UTC,* 73–75, chap. 7)

That is the whole account in a half page, a score of lines in which Eliza the brave young mother was immortalized. Eliza's conduct is instinctive, a woman protecting her offspring; and the further stages of her escape, the scenes with the Birds in Ohio (chap. 9) and the Quakers in Indiana (chap. 13), emphasize the cooperation of women in the cause of family preservation.

Chapter 4 is unique, the only chapter in *Uncle Tom's Cabin* that takes place within "Uncle" Tom's cabin. In the entire book (in an edition of six hundred pages) only twenty-three pages are set within the cabin, and thirteen of these are in Chapter 4. In chapter 5 Eliza comes to the cabin at the start of her escape (three pages), and in chapter 10 Tom bids his wife farewell in ten pages. After that the cabin disappears. In chapter 38 Tom's miserable shack on Legree's plantation is once called "cabin," apparently inadvertently rather than as subtle symbolism, since it is elsewhere described as a shed. The virtual absence of the cabin has led to ingenious explanations of the suitability of its prominence in the title.[2]

Chapter 4 shows the cabin in its glory. Tom is there on an evening with his wife and their three children, the youngest still in arms. Tom seems much younger here than later in the book. Aunt Chloe is exercising her culinary skill and upon occasion "laughing till the tears rolled down her black, shining cheeks." Of all the tears in the book, on sixty different pages, Aunt Chloe's are among the few shed in laughter. The evening has been planned for prayer, and young Mas'r George, an admirable thirteen-year-old, is on hand to help the assembled slaves with their Bible reading and hymn singing. Comical dialect, naive humor, abundant food, and innocent piety combine to depict a kind of life destined for destruction. Tom's departure in chapter 10 is correspondingly sad, and the stoic resignation with which he accepts his separation from his happy family and friends foreshadows the heroism of his last days.

The Central Chapters: St. Clare and Miss Ophelia

How packed with life and action the opening chapters of *Uncle Tom's Cabin* are! Strung together for periodical publication, unlikely and exaggerated, they show one essential gift of the storyteller, an ability to arouse attention. The early reader was eager to know what could happen to Tom and Eliza after they left Kentucky; and greater thrills than before were in store. In the central division of the book, Tom's life with his new masters is contrasted with the protection the refugees find among the Quakers, stouthearted abolitionists. Chronological exactness is discarded here, for while Tom is abiding two years and more with his kind master, Eliza and George do not reach Canada until after the death of St. Clare, though they are hurrying at full speed. Their arrival in Ontario immediately precedes the chapter presaging Tom's Louisiana martyrdom.

In the St. Clare family, inhabitants of a picturesque mansion in New Orleans, Stowe protrays slaveholders at their best. A kind master, a heavenly young mistress, a puzzled Vermont aunt—these line up on the credit side, and against them only a spoiled daughter of wealth, unthinkingly heartless but too indolent to be aggressively cruel. Tom easily adapts himself to his new owner, who recognizes his virtues. In particular is he idolized by Eva, whose life he has saved by hauling her from the Mississippi, a river that might have flowed, as Stowe described it, straight from the exotic pages of Chateaubriand's *Atala* but has never appeared elsewhere to human eyes. Tom might be happy with this owner if it were not for the separation from his family. He is well fed and housed, he has been promised his freedom soon, his Bible reading is encouraged, and he is so highly esteemed that by example he is making progress toward converting his owner to true Christianity. Above all, he and Eva share an ecstatic, mystical love that obliterates all distinctions of race, sex, or social rank. His existence lies in a calm before the final storm precipitated by St. Clare's sudden death.

Meanwhile, shrewdly holding Simon Legree offstage, Stowe delivers her keenest and fairest attack on Negro slavery, the supposed subject of her book. As usual, she puts her criticism into the mouth of one of her characters.

Of all the creations serving this purpose, Augustine St. Clare is the most engaging and the most convincing. A worldling, he has no serious vices, his lack of purpose seeming rather to aid him in viewing life objectively. He is a man who likes to talk, who enjoys being amusing and shocking, and whose principal conversational weapon is a straightforward honesty that his slower-witted auditors mistake for paradox. He is a good fellow, Stowe would have her readers realize, as she apologizes profusely for his frivolity, accounting for it by his unfortunate marriage and his loss, at only thirteen, of his saintly mother. Misfortune's child, he is neither hypocrite nor fool. Stowe compares him to Moore, to Goethe, and to Lord Byron.

With Miss Ophelia, the old-fashioned Calvinist aunt, as interlocutor, St. Clare chatters on at length. He laughs at the prim spinster's discomfort over the familiarities permitted between Tom and Eva.

I know the feeling among some of you northerners well enough. Not that there is a particle of virtue in our not having it; but custom with us does what Christianity ought to do,—obliterates the feeling of personal prejudice. I have often noticed, in my travels north, how much stronger this was with you than with us. You loathe them as you would a snake or a toad, yet you are indignant at their wrongs. You would not have them abused; but you don't want to have anything to do with them yourselves. You would send them to Africa, out of your sight and smell, and then send a missionary or two to do up all the self-denial of elevating them compendiously. Isn't that it? (*UTC,* 208, chap. 16)

The points are well scored. In the more serious mood that seizes him upon occasion, St. Clare expressed strangely proletarian judgments on wage slavery. "Look at the high and the low, all the world over, and it's the same story,—the lower class used up, body, soul, and spirit for the good of the upper." Or this: "The slave-owner can whip his refractory slave to death,—the capitalist can starve him to death." Or this striking parallel to the then recent *Communist Manifesto* of Marx and Engels: "One thing is certain,—that there is a mustering among the masses, the world over; and there is a *dies irae* coming on, sooner or later. The same thing is working in Europe, in England, and in this country" (*UTC,* 270–71, chap. 19).

Incredible as it may seem, the sense of social economic responsibility implied in St. Clare's speeches was utterly foreign to Stowe's thought. Chattel slavery she regarded as iniquitous, and wage slavery as free choice. Never for a moment did she consider the application of St. Clare's ideas to the North. She could denounce the capitalists of monarchical England—some of the English proved unpleasantly sensitive on this point—but she honestly did not know that there existed New England mills in which laborers were working for starvation pay. Quite to the contrary, in her *First Geography for Children* (1855), she held up these factories as special evidence of God's favor.[3]

In St. Clare's speeches Stowe lets him run away from her, and she barely succeeds in bringing him back into the circle of her own ideas by turning his thoughts heavenward. Recalling the millenium promised by his blessed mother, he staggers safely back into the conservative theology of the Beechers and away from the dangers of political radicalism.

Unfortunately for Tom, St. Clare saved is also St. Clare dead. The man's soul is bound for heaven, but Tom is left at the mercy of his frivolous, heartless widow.

Black Topsy, Evangeline, and Simon Legree

If St. Clare's role was profitable fictional property, Topsy's was a gold mine of humor. The wayward slave girl, endowed with the supershowmanship of her race, is equipped by nature to step into the cast of Christy's Ethiopian Minstrels. A challenge to Miss Ophelia's power of discipline, Topsy is used to point to the true moral of the tale—that love is above the law—for only Eva's superhuman love starts Topsy on the path toward decency and honesty.

Chapter 15 has a doubly appropriate title, "Of Tom's New Master, and Various Other Matters," as the "other matters" throughout the book become more obvious in the leisurely account of Tom's two years with the St. Clares. The incidental subjects in chapter 15 include the sanctity of marriage and motherhood, the sinfulness of divorce, the New England character, and the contrasting racial traits of the Negro and "the colder and more correct white race." Much of the discussion, in which the author takes part directly through comments and lecture, is unrelated or only partially related to slavery and abolition. Marie St. Clare, whom Stowe despises, is ridiculed beyond belief and shown to be completely unqualified to be the owner of slaves; indeed, she is as inhuman and vicious as Simon Legree, but her faults are those of misdirected, pampered women everywhere. Similarly, the entertaining and famous confrontation of Miss Ophelia and Topsy is not in essence a contrast of black and white, slave and freeman; it is a comment on twin errors in education—too rigid standards and too little discipline. The same test of wills, between a theory-bound adult and a recalcitrant child, is possible in any setting, except for the pictorial details.

Chapter 17 differs from most of the book in another way: it has incidents written in the manner of an outdoor adventure story, as George Harris, acting like a boy's hero, shoots his evil pursuer. "Down he fell into the chasm, crackling down among trees, bushes, logs, loose stones, till he lay bruised and groaning thirty feet below." Stowe's range of subjects widened as she wrote her serial, and chapter 18 introduces a wretched black woman, Old Prue, whose sudden death, narrated most succinctly, makes one of the most gruesome anecdotes in the book. "Prue, she got drunk agin,—and they had her down cellar,—and thar they left her all day,—and I hearn 'em saying that the flies *had got to her,*—and *she's dead!*" (The italics are Stowe's.)

By this middle section of her book Stowe had not solved all the practical problems of the complicated slave system. From the beginning of its serial publication she championed absolute legal freedom for slaves as a minimum, pointing out on one occasion that George Harris held up his head, speaking and moving like a different man as soon as he regarded himself "free," though at the time he was still doubtful of his safety. Slavery, in its criminal regard of human souls as mere property, was, she thought, a relation different in kind from the woes of ordinary life. Uncle Tom took issue with Stowe, his creator, on this point, for she showed his basic tragedy to be that he was a true Christian among the heathen; and he himself regarded slavery as only one added indignity. A certain "unfashionable old book," from which he read only the New Testament, separated him more completely from his fellow men than either color or servitude.

Tom wanted his freedom, to be sure, as ardently as Stowe wanted it for him; but he preferred slavery and martyrdom to dishonorable flight. He was a black Christ shaming a Yankee Satan. And so, to provide the catharsis of a soul-stirring conclusion, Legree was provided—as cruel a villain as ever dishonored his fair New England origin.

In considering the three sections into which the book is divided, an analyst observes that the first, in its description of the Shelby estate, enriches the tale with verisimilitude, for Stowe had been as far south as Kentucky; the second, in Topsy and St. Clare, with wit and humor; and the third, in Legree, with terror. In Eliza's wild flight, a similar terror appears at the opening of the story, a dramatic foreboding of the powerful conclusion.

As a work of troubled imagination, there is much to be said for *Uncle Tom's Cabin,* aside from its greatness as propaganda. For the episode of Legree particularly, the secluded plantation in the wilderness, the grotesque and cruel inhabitants, the pitiable victims, and the intervention of supernatural powers offer material that neither Anne Radcliffe nor Monk Lewis could have used to better advantage than Stowe.[4] When Tom nobly suffers martyrdom, lingering only long enough to bid farewell to his young master from Kentucky—who has reached him too late to buy his freedom—it is not strange that, in 1852, tears fell upon the pages of the *National Era.* The last few chapters are an anticlimactic device for disposing of the characters as happily as possible; the "Concluding Remarks" of chapter 45, reflections on slavery, is more properly an addendum. The true end of the story comes with the end of Tom in chapter 40, when "Legree, foaming with rage, smote his victim to the ground."

Even so, when the book was completed its success was not nearly as assured as the usual accounts suggest. Abolitionist literature was frankly boycotted by many publishers, and the Stowes secured book publication only after difficult negotiations with an unestablished publisher who would have preferred Stowe to run a large share of the financial risk. If she would contribute five hundred dollars he would pay her a royalty of fifty percent. That the Stowes did not accept this gamble was less a mistake, since they lacked money to risk, than a misfortune for which they suffered the cruelest of penalties. The sales, commencing strong, swelled into thousands and hundreds of thousands. The young publisher's speculation was amply rewarded.

So was Stowe, but her ten percent royalty provided another durable complaint against fate, when she thought of the rejected fifty percent. In the book's success she soon forgot the willingness with which she would have sold her rights for enough money to buy a new silk dress, as her husband had stated his original ambition to her.[5]

Sources

The triumph of *Uncle Tom's Cabin* was more astonishing to the author than she could afterward explain. Her final suggestion, that she had not written it but had taken it in dictation from God, satisfied her in her old age. Before reaching this solution, she had been inclined to take most of the credit herself, with an assist from Henry Ward's promise to scatter her still-unwritten words thick as the leaves of Vallombrosa. Or perhaps, as she believed in 1870, she had been driven to write it, like her other books, "by the necessity of making some income for family expenses." Nor could she decide exactly where or when she had started to write and whether the death of Uncle Tom was the first or the last part of the book to be set down.

Among the least convincing attempts to explain the mystery is the suggestion, later accepted in her son's official biography of her, that the novel was slowly evolved, thought over as a long-planned contribution to the abolition movement. During the long years of antislavery activity in which she did no writing for the cause, Stowe may well have been personally disturbed; but she remained socially unawakened and publicly uncommitted. She joined none of the groups urging government action, neither the radical abolitionists not the idealistic Quakers, whom she eulogized in the novel. She was a private person, unqualified in her own estimation for public action until she was swept up into the northern moral revolt against the Fugitive Slave Law of 1850.

How many of the events and characters of *Uncle Tom's Cabin* were taken directly from Stowe's life is problematic, but undoubtedly many were. Before Harriet's birth, the Beechers had known black persons in New England as house servants, and Harriet had memories of tales about them heard in her childhood. In Cincinnati, slavery was such a prominent issue, with slaves so close by, that only a hermit could have remained uninformed. The experiences of her brother Charles, who had worked in Louisiana, and her brother Edward, who had lived through riots in Illinois, were as vivid to her from their accounts as if they were her own. In short, she knew a great deal about slavery through her family, not in terms of an economic system but as details and anecdotes that sound convincing in a story.

Written sources have been identified for parts of *Uncle Tom's Cabin*. The autobiography of Josiah Henson, an escaped slave who later became famous as the original of Uncle Tom, is one of these. His idealistic character was congenial to her, many of his traits finding their way into her depiction of Tom. Undoubted as his services to her were, their exact extent is disputable. In one respect these two were alike: for while Henson was inclined to exaggerate his helpfulness, Stowe considered her generosity ample when she referred to his published autobiography as "an exemplification of the truth of the character of her Uncle Tom." According to Henson, however, he supplied her with the originals of George Harris and Eliza, who were his particular friends; of Topsy, who was as near like a certain Dinah on his old plantation as one pea to another; of Simon Legree in the person of Bryce Litton, "who broke my arms and marred me for life"; and also of St. Clare and Eva, in the persons of Mr. St. Clair Young and his daughter.

Except for George Harris, in these identifications Henson was mistaken. To the limited degree that Eliza was drawn from life, rather than from Stowe's suffering, she was either a fugitive whom Calvin Stowe and Henry Ward Beecher had helped, or she was, according to another family explanation, the subject of an account in an antislavery paper. The human original of Topsy was a Negro girl, Celeste by name, known to the family in Cincinnati. The character of Legree, which seems to have been both fathered and mothered by writers of melodramas, is said to have been sketched for her by her brother Charles. The original of Eva was her own dead daughter, who was also later to serve as model for Tina in *Oldtown Folks*.[6]

Other narratives by slaves lay at hand for rapid reading, so numerous and accessible that Stowe could not have missed all of them. Frances Smith Foster, who has studied six thousand for her book *Witnessing Slavery: The Development of Ante-bellum Slave Narratives* (1979), has found striking similarities among them, incidents from life that also appear, told more appealingly, in *Uncle Tom's Cabin*. Chapter 5 of Foster's book, "The Plot of Ante-bellum Slave Narratives" (Westbrook, Conn.: Greenwood Press, 1979; 82–126) a composite of many autobiographies, analyzes familiar common elements: (1) a calm pastoral period; (2) the separation of families; (3) the hypocrisy of professing Christians; (4) horrible working conditions; (5) floggings and beatings, with descriptions of the whips and other instruments of torture; and (6) escape to Canada or some other promised land.

One book to which Stowe admitted her indebtedness is Theodore Weld's *American Slavery as It Is* (1839). Her debt to Weld is greater than to any of her Negro informants, and perhaps greater than she understood. Weld, whom she had known years before, had been a brilliant student at Lane Seminary early in Lyman Beecher's presidency. An abolitionist even in 1834, Weld had been threatened with expulsion as a troublemaker; instead he had withdrawn from school, taking with him ninety-two others—"he-goat men," according to Beecher, "butting everything in the line of their march which does not fall or get out of their way"—and reducing the enrollment of Lane Seminary from an even one hundred students to seven.[7]

One of the best known propaganda books about abolition, *American Slavery as It Is* is an accumulation of newspaper clippings with appropriate comments. In Stowe's preface to the 1878 *Uncle Tom's Cabin* she acknowledged her use of the book and privately, to Weld's wife, Angelina Grimke, she went handsomely beyond her public testimony in her description of how "she kept that book in her work basket by day, and slept with it under her pillow by night, till its facts crystallized into Uncle Tom."[8]

In addition to such recognized obligations to Weld, Henson, and other agitators, Stowe's story shares obvious similarities with other abolitionist and plantation fiction. Although she nowhere indicates acquaintance with earlier antislavery novels, the situations and characters of both *Uncle Tom's Cabin* and *Dred* are partly traditional. In Richard Hildreth's *The Slave; or, Memoirs of Archy Moore* (1836), the best written example of the type, the cruel overseer is a Yankee like Legree; Archy himself has the same combination of pride and sensitive feelings as George Harris, Eliza's husband; an easygoing squire with eighteenth-century liberal ideas is a possible, but not realized, St. Clare; and his son is the exact double of Tom Gordon in *Dred,* "a tyrant from whose soul custom had long since obliterated what little human-ity nature had bestowed upon him."[9] Stowe had probably never seen *The Slave* before she wrote *Uncle Tom's Cabin,* but the possibilities were limitless for picking up suggestions from antislavery novels or from more popular novels dwelling on the attractive side of plantation life.[10]

Of all the sources of *Uncle Tom's Cabin,* the most decisive is one least considered, the periodical for which it was written, whose policies were implicit in the shaping of the story. Here, as always, Stowe was writing for an editor and a public whose expectations she could not disregard. More than the author knew, her story was nourished, during its long period of serial publication, on the spirit of the *National Era* itself.

The *National Era* first appeared on 7 January 1847, with Gamaliel Bailey as editor and John Greenleaf Whittier as one of the associates. From the start it expressed determined antislavery principles, but it was not exclusively a propaganda sheet. It reported congressional de-bates from its first issue, and it soon printed an appeal for the Irish poor, several articles favoring temperance, full accounts of the French revolution of 1848, and a news story on the woman's rights convention of the same year. Further removed from such reforming activities, it ran an enthusiastic account of Jenny Lind, written by Fredrika Bremer, as well as an editorial on the same vocal artist; and reviews of books and magazines were a regular department.

On the whole, the magazine justified its stated aim: "to mingle literature with politics . . . and to keep both subordinate to the great movement on behalf of human liberty." It was easy to read and no doubt effective. When Garrison's *Liberator* denounced Bailey's *Era* as "milk and water," the editor replied that "we take our stand as far South as we can," and "appeal to the Southern people as men of like passions with ourselves" (22 July 1847; 14 December 1848).

Though the *Era* was conciliatory in intent, it occasionally described horrors, such as the lashing and torturing of a maid mistakenly sus-pected of stealing from her owner. Her last words were, however, the meat of the account. "Let me say my prayers before I die" (2 September 1847). In this item, as throughout the magazine, the appeal was funda-mentally moral. Many stories by E. D. E. N. Southworth were used, with the editorial recommendation, "We need not say with what effect Mrs. Southworth uses fiction as a vehicle of truth."[11]

Southworth's serials, such as *Pride* and *Retribution,* were not abolitionist, for it was Bailey's policy to provide original sketches and tales for home reading along with his political agitation. This was the need that Stowe was also expected to serve, as a young expert in the domestic and the moral. Of her four contributions before *Uncle Tom's Cabin,* only one mentioned the slavery issue. This was the first, a token of her antislavery sympathies, "The Freeman's Dream: A Parable," restating the editor's view that the laws of God were above the constitution of the United States. After this goodwill offering, she sent "A Scholar's Adventures in the Country," a mild satire against the impractical man; "Christmas, or the Good Fairy"; and "Independence," a story directed against nighttime parties. All of these, printed between 1 August 1850 and 30 January 1851, were the type of mild sketch she had been doing for years; only on 2 June 1851 did her serial begin, preceded by an editorial announcement of 8 May 1851.

What had occurred in the meantime to turn her attention from late parties and impractical philologists was, of course, the Fugitive Slave Act.[12] The *National Era* itself was full of stories and editorials denouncing it, beginning as early as 26 September 1850. In the issue of 26 December, the first page of the paper was shared by the Christmas story and a discussion of the act of Congress. On 2 January 1851 Whittier wrote against it. On 5 June it was discussed on the same page with the first installment of *Uncle Tom's Cabin;* and after that date, as before, it was a burning issue with both editors and contributors, who feared it as much as they hated it. These were days in which even a small boy like Henry James observed that "the question of what persons of colour might or mightn't do was intensely in the air";[13] and along with the hothouse atmosphere of Stowe's excited writing on the serial, the weekly fuel supplied by the *Era* contributed more than a mite to the increased emotion of later installments.

Uncle Tom's Cabin; or, the Man That Was a Thing, to use the original subtitle, began on 5 June 1851 and was concluded on 1 April 1852. In all this period, Stowe missed only two installments, a good record for the *National Era.* By 30 October 1851, the fan mail was beginning, with a letter making suggestions about future book publication. Shortly afterward the editor stated that "nearly all our readers" were showing great interest in the tale—this was directly after the death of Eva, which had been spread over four installments, from 20 November to 11 December 1851. Book publication was announced on 25 March 1852, and by the end of that week, when the final chapter appeared in the *National Era,* literary history was being made on a wider scale.

After *Uncle Tom's Cabin,* Stowe's relationship with the *National Era* was not close. She sent a few short original pieces, including a moral tale, "Don't You Like Flowers?," an article on temperance in Maine and a plea to the Presbyterian church to take a strong antislavery stand. Her further association was mostly through reprints and the magazine's comments on the triumphal progress of *Uncle Tom's Cabin.* For an entire year the paper was filled with praises of her and replies to her detractors. [14]

Harriet Beecher Stowe reaped incalculable advantage from her contract with the *National Era.* It was as essential to her as the Fugitive Slave Act itself. Left to a normal development, a mild interest in freedom for the blacks could have produced only further water and milk sketches like "Immediate Emancipation" or "The Freeman's Dream." On the other hand, absolute frenzy over abolition would have got nowhere with *Godey's Lady's Book* or the other carefully noncommittal magazines of her apprenticeship. The *National Era* lent the ideal encouragement to her expanded efforts, never shocking her as the *Liberator* did, yet exerting steady pressure toward writing about freedom. Not only did it furnish her with a commercial outlet, without which she never wrote; more important, it fed her with indignation and fury, and on occasion with details for the advancement of her story. Its absorption in the wrongs of an enslaved race was a tremendous help to her: by taking her mind from petty domestic problems it allowed her suppressed sense of her own servitude to identify itself with the most widely appealing issue of the day. [15] The added circumstance that the *Era* had no standard of literary attitudinizing that she felt compelled to follow was not the least of its services to her, since it allowed her to write freely for a definite public of sympathetic readers. [16]

Chapter Four
The Years Between

A Key to "Uncle Tom's Cabin" (1853)

Sensational success though it was, both *Uncle Tom's Cabin* and its author were attacked from many quarters. During several years of intense national political stress, Stowe as controversial public figure encountered criticism to which as housewife she had been totally unaccustomed. That she should reply indignantly is not surprising, as she did in her next book of explanation, *A Key to "Uncle Tom's Cabin."*[1]

The charges against her ranged from ignorance and poor writing to unfeminine conduct, impiety, malice, and greed. A particular irritant was a London *Times* review stating that her novel could appeal only to readers with strong hearts and weak intellects.[2] Personal attacks, some of them scurrilous, were common, as when a South Carolina poet, William J. Grayson, denounced her, in sturdy heroic couplets, as "a moral scavenger" who "sniffs up pollution with a pious air . . . and trades for gold the garbage of her toils."[3]

With such provocation, Stowe's public response in her *Key* was a restrained rebuttal of the objective charges of ignorance and inaccuracy, with only background hints of personal resentment. Starting as a twenty-five page appendix to the novel, it grew into an entire book, defending and reiterating her depiction of slavery as a moral evil. What was immediately apparent to friends and foes alike in this sizeable volume, written in fulfillment of a promise to present the "original facts and documents" on which her novel was based, was the limitation of her original data.

For example, she indicates surprise in reading in the New York *Courier and Enquirer* an article stating that in Louisiana, where Tom was supposed to have been whipped to death and a young slave girl publicly sold from her mother, both incidents could never have occurred openly, since both were acts that the laws of the state declared criminal and punished as such. The writer of this article also took issue with Stowe on another point dear to her heart, proving that the privation of religious instruction, as she had described it, was "utterly unfounded in fact," and citing the first African churches in Louisville and Augusta, with memberships of fifteen hundred and thirteen hundred respectively, as specimens of churches entirely of, by, and for the slaves (*Key,* 125).

Though Stowe might protest this author's personal judgment against her book—"a ridiculously extravagant spirit of generalization pervades this fiction from beginning to end"—she could not fail to realize that it identified the gaps in her information (*Key,* 125). Answer him directly she could not, for the facts were his; reply to him she could, for her corroborative evidence, supplied by hundreds of correspondents and found in southern newspapers, revealed to her the full horror of the dispersion of black families and the human tragedy of black slavery as she had imagined them.

Knowing the humiliation of subservience from her own childhood, she was on her true ground when she wrote, echoing Theodore Weld's ringing challenge, that "the deadly sin of slavery is its denial of humanity to man" (*Key,* 242). From this point of view, she could continue the argument begun in her novel: if the Negro is a man, what possible excuse can there be for denying him liberty and equality?

Though the *Key* did nothing to enhance Stowe's reputation as a novelist, it was a step forward in her public career. It demonstrated her determination as a debater and strengthened her importance in the antislavery movement. The first fourteen chapters, a commentary on her novel, offer convincing evidence that characters like the Shelbys and the St. Clares, even Tom and Legree, were drawn partly from life, that she knew some of them herself and had read about others in accounts of unquestionable accuracy. Having made this point, she moved ahead to her more important subject, the evils of slavery, in thirty-five chapters of examples, the majority of which had come to her attention after her novel had been published. The advertisements from southern newspapers for sales of likely young male and female slaves and the rewards offered for escaped slaves are persuasive.

The *Key* is good propaganda, directed at a much smaller group of readers than the novel. The final chapter, "What Is to Be Done?," is addressed exclusively to "the whole American church," demanding an unequivocal denunciation of slavery. Stowe foresaw no hope from government, national or local, and fervent prayer was the only weapon she proposed.

Dred (1856)

If the writing of *Uncle Tom's Cabin* was like an unavoidable explosion and the writing of the *Key to "Uncle Tom's Cabin"* like an unavoidable argument, the next book in the series, *Dred: A Tale of the Great Dismal Swamp,* took form as an unavoidable literary obligation. A second antislavery novel was obviously Stowe's duty to her public and her publishers. My "whole mind was wrought up in the story," she told one of her publishers, "and [I] would pace the floor late at night dictating to [my] amanuensis."[4] Though freedom might be further away than ever, after the subsiding enthusiasm of the fugitive slave days there was still opportunity for antislavery fiction.[5]

To the author, the initial reception of *Dred* was more than satisfactory. After four years of the golden publicity of controversy, the new novel was off to a better early sale than its predecessor. Soon Stowe was able to ask significantly, as the royalties began to pour in on her, "After that who cares what the critics say?" (AF, 222).

That question might still be asked, now that time has thrust *Dred* into the stacks of forgotten novels from which *Uncle Tom's Cabin* has been miraculously separated. Stylistically no better than the other, *Dred* lacked the essential breath of life. It was too largely what it purported to be, a book about black slaves and their white owners at home, less inspiring subjects than fugitive and suffering women. Forty years of repression were worth more for insight into injustice than the three or four years of study and writing that went into *Dred*.

Even in the narrow aspect of craftsmanship the comparative weakness of *Dred* can be understood. The story has a very slow beginning, presenting a scatterbrained young woman who has become engaged to three men, none of whom she intends to marry. The next two chapters present a young man and his family. The fourth chapter returns to the girl's family, including a glance at its historical beginnings a century back. The succeeding chapters continue the panorama, until in the eighteenth chapter Dred himself appears.

Some of the pictures are fine, the plantation very clear, and a death scene and funeral services very affecting, but much of the detail is irrelevant to the narrative. The literary tone ranges from the light chatter of the ladies magazines to solid exposition suited to editorials in the *Independent*. Throughout the book the different kinds of material are poorly fitted together. In spite of the documentary evidence from Nat Turner's narrative, submitted in the appendix, the romantic paraphernalia is used unabashed; and Dred himself, the prophetic leader of his race, is, except for the detail of pigmentation, a hero from Scottish literature, a wild chieftan fleeing to an inaccessible stronghold from which he has sallied forth to confound the oppressors of his people. His conversation, a melange of biblical passages, is a continuous, intense declamation; and at the sound of his voice, invisibly carried through the night air, even heartless slave owners tremble, conscious of their sins.

For a time, as the story develops, hints are offered that Stowe will counsel the slaves to arise and slay the tyrants—as John Brown was later to attempt and as Professor Stowe had once urged in a moment of excitement—but timely reflection led her to an alternative solution through a saintly death for her hero. His dying, as noble as his living, suggests the inadequacy of force in solving a problem that she continued to regard as primarily religious.

Around an utterly fantastic core of swamp-girdled retreats and mysterious, handy sorties, she conducts a more realistic discussion of a subject that was still among her main interests: "the degenerate Christianity of the slave states" (*Dred,* vol. 2, 22). To her there was constant wonder in the loyalty of the southern clergy to their social institutions. They must be fools or knaves, she was sure, and through her pages she conducts a veritable parade of reverend gentlemen defending slavery or protesting that nothing can be done to abolish it. The nonconformist Dickson, single exception to the worldliness and wickedness of his brethren, is rewarded for his outspokenness with insults and violence. Naturally enough, the northern clergymen are also taken to task, for they were still, in spite of her *Key,* shirking their duty.

Accompanying these discussions of the religious situation, Stowe attempted a survey of the economic life of the South. As she had never been in the Carolinas, the scene of her story, she was compelled to depend on items in the *National Era*—most of which originated in Virginia— republished court records, and information volunteered by others sharing her views. Despite such difficulties, she succeeded in introducing a wide variety of recognizable types: the prosperous, kindly plantation owner; the poorer owner, more kindly still, forced by necessity to dispose of his human property; the vicious, drunken, lustful debauchee to whom she was pleased to refer as the flower of southern chivalry "adept in every low form of vice" (*Dred,* vol. 1, 46); the poor white, a coarse creature spiritually debased by competition with unpaid labor.

Conventional though these characters are, the whites in *Dred* exhibit more diversity than the blacks, for the former have the choice of being good or bad, while the latter have apparently all been created virtuous, predestination arranging only a difference in suffering.

This sociological romancing, along with the theological tracting, is strung on the unsubstantial cord of a love story. In Stowe's philosophy of fiction, a novel meant a few pages of such startling action as lynchings and cholera epidemics, sandwiched between generous portions of unprogressing discussion. There is just such a spasmodic action in *Dred,* less successfully managed than in *Uncle Tom's Cabin* because of its triviality in comparison with the great causes associated with it. The love affair between a "princess of little flirts," Nina Gordon, and the idealistic master of four hundred slaves, Edward Clayton, meant so little to the author herself that she disposed of her heroine with two hundred pages of her story left, so that her hero would be free to devote his undivided attention to his Negro brethren. Nina Gordon's beautiful death might have appealed more strongly to the feelings if little Eva had not died so much more appealingly and if poor Sue Cripps, wife of a brutal poor white, had not, in this very book, preceded her into the great beyond with vivid economy.

Throughout *Dred,* the hard-pressed author was haunted by memories of *Uncle Tom's Cabin.* Thus Harry Gordon, a superior young slave, is Eliza's husband almost to a tittle, and Tomtit is their boy who is carried across the river. Old Tiff, a faithful retainer, is not Uncle Tom and Nina's Aunt Nesbit is not precisely Miss Ophelia, although her function in the story is the same; but the minor slave characters in North Carolina are duplicates of those in *Uncle Tom's Cabin.* As miscegenation is one of the major villains in *Dred,* Tom Gordon, who hates his black half-brother, is as satanic as Legree in the author's intention, though not in her execution.

Ineptly as some details of her story are arranged, *Dred* shows Stowe's courage in facing the discouraging task of abolition. Although her story ends happily for the survivors, with a final chapter called "Clear Shining after Rain," she saw no hope for emancipation. Edward Clayton, who freed his slaves, is as untypical as Uncle Tom. Given the indifference of the North and the political entrenchment of the South, the best that could be done for slaves was to get them out of the slave states into the neat tenements of New York and the gemlike Gothic cottages of New England. Millie and Uncle Tiff are happy in these surroundings (without mention of plans for colonization in Africa); and Tomtit has " 'come a Christian, a jined the church; and they has him to wait and tend at the antislavery office." It is remarkable that of all the gifts Stowe wanted for the Negroes—the social and moral values of New Englanders, plus their own jolly dancing—the one that they would first receive, legal emancipation, was the one that she least anticipated. John Brown's raid and the election of a Republican president were essential contributing events yet in the future.[6]

Sunny Memories of Foreign Lands (1854)

Success never spoiled Stowe. Criticism or opposition irritated her, but once it was overcome she regained her composure and solicitude for all mankind. To soften the furious controversies of the 1850s she sought relaxation in European travel. The first of her three vacation trips was so memorable that she perpetuated it in a two-volume work, *Sunny Memories of Foreign Lands,* which consisted of her published "letters" to the *Independent* magazine, a preface by her husband, and several chapters supplied by her brother Charles, another member of the party, who kept a private diary, published many years later, confirming the success of the expedition.

From one point of view it was not much of a trip, the stereotyped grand tour of Great Britain, France, Germany, Switzerland, and Belgium, but it gave her more pleasure than she had known, in the respect and adoration of those who met her. Guidebook in hand, following Walter Scott through Scotland and Martin Luther through Germany, she enjoyed even the conventional round of inspection; and between the visits to cathedrals and ragged schools, there were stupendous gatherings in her honor.

Wherever she went, in Great Britain particularly, celebrities assembled at the dinners and receptions held for her. Macaulay, Gladstone, Dickens, Sir William Hamilton, Lady Byron, and Mrs. Jameson were a few of those she met and commented on freely in her letters. But greatly as the literary men aroused her curiosity, and much as the sturdy peasants and the honest Liverpool laborers pleased her with their Christian character, she found her greatest delight in meeting the aristocracy. With gusto she entered into her letters the splendid titles of duke and duchess, lord and lady, marquis and marchioness. With some of them she exhibited a good deal of interest in reform movements, such as prohibition in Scotland; but one of her greatest delights was a concert concerning which she wrote to her husband: "Well, the Hons. and Right Hons. all were there. I sat by Lord Carlisle."

After leaving England, she was given more opportunity to rest and to recover strength sapped out of her by her hospitable British hosts. She was more critical of what she found on the mainland, sunny as her memories were. She was dissatisfied with the collection at the Louvre, looking in vain for pictures "great and glorious enough to seize and control my whole being." Catholic cathedrals distressed her Protestant soul with their "horrible and loathesome idolatry" and their poor worshippers "kneeling, with clasped hands and bowed heads, praying with an earnestness which was sorrowful to see." Even the Swiss Alps threatened to fail her, because so many of them were simply stones until she found Mont Blanc; and patriotism led her to prefer Niagara to it.[7]

No wonder she had a good time. On her return home, she brought not only her sunny memories and her keepsakes, her pebbles from the Tweed, testimonials from co-workers and a volume of sermons given her by the archbishop of Canterbury, "relating to the elevation and christianization of the masses." More than these precious knickknacks, she brought home a new tolerance for others, a special love for England, "kind-strong old England—the Mother of us All," and a realization that the French are not incapable of religious feeling. Worried as she was that her admiration for chivalry and feudalism was perhaps inconsistent with the spirit of Christ, she had been so often thrilled by beauty that criticism of the Puritans as lacking in aesthetic appreciation took on a new, stronger meaning for her.

Stowe's second visit to Europe, an event of 1856, though equally successful, was more pleasant because less formal and exhausting than her first grand tour. With her pleasure trip she combined the satisfying business of securing British copyright for *Dred*, to protect her royalties; and the enormous sale of the book, in England as in America, she interpreted as a token of the favor of God, who was bestowing upon her more of this world's goods than she had dared ask in her prayers. For her regular journalistic work, she sent public letters like *Sunny Memories* to her magazine, the *Independent*.

With her international royalties safe and her reputation in the ascendant, she lightheartedly renewed her old acquaintances among the aristocracy and formed some new attachments. From the duchess of Sutherland she received gratifying news: the queen herself was eagerly reading *Dred*, which, as later communications revealed, she ranked above *Uncle Tom's Cabin*. It was on this trip that Stowe enjoyed three happy days at the home of Charles Kingsley, where she was astonished to learn that the literary divine was a zealous Anglican. When she visited Ruskin, it was the Englishman's turn to be astonished, in the first place because she preferred "going in a boat on the river" to examining the notable manuscripts of Durham, and in the second place because there was no river fit for boating, but only a trickle about as big as "a not very large town drain."[8]

There were no major literary results of this second European jaunt, but on her third and last visit abroad (1859), during the final happy stage passed in Italy, she not only sent lengthy dispatches to the *Independent* but also began a historical novel, *Agnes of Sorrento*. These were indeed happy days, during which she lived gloriously on the success of *Uncle Tom's Cabin* and *Dred*. Of her new friends, the most important to her was Annie Fields, wife of the Boston publisher and later her capable biographer.

During these active, productive years, when her moral indignation was riding high, the only overwhelming sorrow to disturb her sense of wholesome achievement was the death, in 1857, of her eldest son, Henry. The boy, a freshman at Dartmouth College, died suddenly of drowning, and to the natural bereavement of a mother was added the ancient fear of damnation; for Henry had not been formally saved. "I may not be what the world calls a Christian," he had written, "but I will live such a life as every true man ought to live" (AF, 240). Alas! Might his virtuous behavior be perhaps not enough? Was his death not similar to Professor Fisher's, about which Catherine had never reassured herself completely? Might he not, as she had been taught by her father, be damned?

Through this crisis of doubt Stowe returned amazingly to girlhood fears that success had banished. She composed a complete account of her affliction for the duchess of Sutherland and another for her daughters in Paris. To her sister Catherine she confessed that the old temptations of the devil assailed her; and her soul hung in the balance as she feared that her trust in God had been misplaced. When at length she had recovered her faith in Jesus, she was greatly pleased by her husband's visions, in which Henry's presence returned, accompanied by the vibrations of a mysterious guitar. More comforting still was the final explanation agreed on between them that the guitar, since Henry was no musician, must have been struck by Eliza, the professor's first wife (AF, 153; CES, 350).

The direct literary results of the vacation travels of these middle years, the book *Sunny Memories* and her public correspondence, are revelatory rather than intrinsically valuable. She was alert and vivacious, but her double handicap as traveler was inexperience and a lack of caution.

Men of Our Times (1868)

Men of Our Times is a difficult book to place in a survey of Stowe's publications. Its subject links it to *Uncle Tom's Cabin* (1852) and *Dred* (1856), to the extent that the Civil War is related to slavery and emancipation. The date of publication, however, places *Men of Our Times* closer to *Oldtown Folks* (1869) and subsequent to *The Minister's Wooing* (1859) and other books with which it has no similarities. No mystery is involved, for *Men of Our Times* is a collection of earlier magazine articles reissued in 1868 as a subscription book for door-to-door sale, a memorial of the war years. The biographical sketches were probably at their freshest in their original appearance in a Baptist paper, the *Watchman and Reflector*.

Aside from her writing, Stowe's personal contributions to winning the Civil War were indirect. Her second son, Frederick William, was among the earliest volunteers, and his services, including promotion in rank and permanent injury at Gettysburg, offered the glamour of story-book heroism as well as an opportunity for personal intercession on his behalf with military and political authorities. The solemnity of the great public gatherings thrilled her, and like other civilians she was "inspirited" by the military music "in which the soldiers joined with hearty voices" (AF, 260). She responded wholeheartedly to the appeal of cheering people, of waving handkerchiefs, of fine-looking army chaplains, and especially to the delirium of a religious festival in the capital city at which a thousand redeemed slaves prayed and sang hymns.

Such excitement was in itself almost too strenuous for her, but it was pleasant, whereas her private life, continuing in the habitual flurry of nervousness, was filled with trouble. Existence was further complicated by several changes in residence, first from Andover to Hartford, Connecticut, when her husband retired from teaching, and later within the city of Hartford, when after two years the house built to her bizarre specifications was abandoned because of the intrusion of industry into the neighborhood. The wedding of her daughter reduced her, as she phrased it, to "sheer imbecility"; and other domestic exigencies kept her continually worried and discontented.

She found, nevertheless, much to arouse that sense of moral indignation that she esteemed a chief among the virtues. From time to time

arose such crises as the impudent question asked by the Congregationalist ministers of England as to why the North did not let the South go.
And there were always, in otherwise dull moments, the "horrible
barbarities" of the southern soldiers. As her specific war services, she
wrote essays for the *Independent* and the *Atlantic Monthly* on the prosecu-
tion of the campaign, patriotic poems about the war to end war, as well
as an important "Appeal to the Women of England," in reply to an
address she had received from them some eight years previously.[9] Amid
the desolate hearths and ruined homesteads of which she spoke, she was
sustained by the knowledge that she was assisting at "the throes and
ravings of the exorcism" of slavery, and the conclusion of the war left
her spiritually satisfied if physically depleted. As though to emphasize
the final ascendancy of the North, she moved, as soon as was
practical—that is, in 1868—to Florida, where she could examine first-
hand the work of Reconstruction and firmly guide the freedmen toward
New England virtue.

On one principle she finally agreed with William Lloyd Garrison,
who had declared in closing the books of the Anti-Slavery Society, that
slavery was ended. The Emancipation Proclamation satisfied her moral
sense, and she was willing to allow as long a time as necessary for the
full absorption of the Negro into political life. She looked forward
calmly to an indefinite period during which brother Henry Ward and
others of "moral influence" were to win over the "really good men" of
the South. What to do with the former slaves in the new South was a
problem she considered in articles for the *North American Review* and
other magazines, but she realized that a solution was beyond her powers. Brooding over the situation, she could do nothing better in *Men of
Our Times* than fight again through the Civil War, still temperamen-
tally in the midst of the combat.

Although she assembled it hastily from previous magazine articles,
and almost unwillingly except for the money it would bring, Stowe
thought well of this book. It would be good for young men and women
to read, she was sure. She rather overestimated it, however, for her
eighteen biographical sketches are colorless and uninspiring.

Men of Our Times is a thoroughly provincial book. Stowe was dread-
fully in earnest in expounding the careers of the "leading patriots of the
day," as a subtitle designated them: the statesmen, generals, and ora-
tors whose high morality had demolished the "so-styled Southern aristocracy." These patriots included Lincoln; Grant; Garrison; Charles
Sumner; Salmon P. Chase; Henry Wilson, "the self-taught, fearless

shoe-maker's apprentice of Natick" who became governor of Massachusetts; Greeley; Farragut; John Andrew, "a consistently Christian State governor" of Connecticut; Colfax, speaker of the House; Stanton; Frederick Douglass, escaped slave and professional lecturer for the Anti-Slavery Society; generals Sheridan, Sherman, and Howard; William A. Buckingham, another governor of Connecticut; Wendell Phillips; and Henry Ward Beecher.

Of these sketches, only the last has intrinsic worth. Stowe interpreted her brother with sisterly devotion, exulting in his every triumph, and sympathizing with such foibles as his abandonment of an interest in mathematics and the classics in favor of an abiding passion for phrenology. His opposition to tobacco and gin echoed her own. And she regarded his invention of a circular study table with a hole in the middle as an especially happy manifestation of a mind equipped to solve difficult problems.

After her brother, she particularly praised Grant, whose statesmanship impressed her as deeply as his military skill, and Charles Sumner, the New England Brahmin whose advocacy of legal abolition contrasted favorably in her mind with the fanatical agitation of Garrison.[10] Abraham Lincoln, though honored in the opening and longest sketch, was not one of her favorites; and there was scarcely concealed uneasiness in her reference to his "queer stories" and other traits incomprehensible to a New England lady.

Insofar as *Men of Our Times* has a subject, it is the achievement of a Christian democracy. The rebellion, which she regarded as the fulfillment of biblical prophecy, was her villain. Recognizing that slavery was but one type of injustice, she occasionally reminded her readers of the dangers of drink, tobacco, and dancing. She did indeed show, as she had promised, the racial histories of her men (over half were New Englanders, over one-third were direct lineal descendants of the Puritans); but she badly neglected consideration of the characters and influence of mothers; with Garrison alone did she rise to the full height of her opportunities.

With *Men of Our Times* Stowe bade farewell to the questions of slavery and rebellion that had inspired a series of books beginning with *Uncle Tom's Cabin*. One may agree that the enslavement of human beings is a sin and a crime that needed to be proclaimed with vigor and persistence. If such was the purpose for which life had prepared her, she had performed it, in some two thousand pages of print, with commendable completeness.

Chapter Five

Mother, Home, and Household Sermons

The literary activity of Stowe's maturity was stupendous. Advancing her money-making career, she continued writing for magazines at a steady grind, with long and short stories and articles composed at breakneck speed. Within eleven years of the publication of *Dred* she wrote eleven books, including three of her most substantial novels, and in the ten years after that she published fourteen more, ending with *Poganuc People* (1878). Eventually then, at sixty-seven, she was forced to take the rest she had so long needed, a rest that proved to be permanent retirement. Her public hated to see her go, and as late as 1883 the rumor was spread that she was planning another novel, to be called *Orange Blossoms*—a rumor that she definitely, almost brusquely, denied.

During these productive years she wrote on a miscellany of subjects, from Byron to the Bible, eighteenth-century New England to modern New York and Florida, in poems, stories, and essays, for men, women, and children. Only by close examination can these writings be gathered into two groups, amorphous at best, one with a New England background, the other dealing with domestic life in the Reconstruction period. The more important group, a continuation of the early regional sketches, includes primarily five books: *The Minister's Wooing, The Pearl of Orr's Island, Oldtown Folks, Sam Lawson's Oldtown Fireside Stories*, and *Poganuc People*. To these should be added, as pendants in contrast, *Agnes of Sorrento* and *Palmetto-Leaves*, both of which describe civilizations alien to that which held her greatest loyalty.

The second amorphous group, dealing with social life—a continuation of the early moral sketches—includes three volumes of essays, beginning with *House and Home Papers*, the three remaining novels, beginning with *My Wife and I*, and the treatise *The American Woman's Home*. With them belong also two books on religion, which are in effect studies in the practical applications of religion in Reconstruction America. The book on Byron, because of the important influence of Byron on

Stowe's entire life, deserves individual analysis. The children's stories, also unaccounted for in this twofold division, can be disregarded without serious consequences, except as they add a touch of fantasy not exhibited elsewhere in her works: for the most part they contain the same ideas as her books for adults, with much the same expression.

Her Americanism was absolute, with three centers of interest and concern: the late eighteenth and early nineteenth centuries in New England, the years of antislavery agitation, and the troubled postwar years of rampant commercialism. In her stories, early and late, she earnestly protested against the extremes of strict Calvinism. Her opposition to slavery, which grew from protest to denunciation, diminished again, after legal emancipation, into protest against lingering injustice. In the postwar years she wrote as a celebrity about the newly developing difficulties in living right. Since she lacked the power of constructive planning, she offered no program such as Christian Socialism, embraced by idealists like Howells and Edward Everett Hale; but her writings, though indecisive, are worth examining as social and personal documents.

Religious Tracts

With a father, a husband, and seven brothers in the ministry, a woman would think about religion, whatever she might say before her men folks. For Harriet Beecher Stowe, to think was to speak out strong, bold, and often. With her faith that all problems are religious, she did not feel that turning her attention from God to human society was a departure from her professed subject. Thus a sentence on urban crime is not out of place in a chapter on "The Attractiveness of Jesus." "We know there are in all our cities desperate and perishing classes inhabiting regions where it would be hardly safe for a reputable person to walk."[1] Two books, *Woman in Sacred History* (1873) and *Footsteps of the Master* (1877), as direct statements of her final religious beliefs, show how far she had moved from the grim doctrines forced on her as a child.[2]

The relationship between God and man was, the evidence indicates, her preoccupation throughout life. Her earliest triumph as a schoolgirl writer was won with a composition entitled "Can the Immortality of the Soul Be Proved by the Light of Nature?" Her answer, at the age of twelve, was a clear *no*. "Never till the blessed light of the Gospel dawned on the borders of the pit and the heralds of the Cross proclaimed 'Peace on earth and good will to men,' was it that bewildered and misled man was enabled to trace his celestial origin and glorious destiny."[3]

Holding undeviatingly to this childhood conviction, she devoted an appalling number of pages to puzzling over the precise attributes demanded of the finest type of God. Her religious thinking was a special pride; her reflections upon godhood were both her greatest comfort and her firmest conviction that she had something valuable to say.

Granting that there was more of the conventional or traditional in her beliefs than she realized, one need not attempt to answer categorically the question, How much of a Puritan was she? By the nineteenth century, the Yankees having succeeded them, there were no true Puritans, but Lyman Beecher must have been as near an approach to the classic models as was humanly possible. Stowe was not entirely true to type, for the great Puritans were intellectual, not sentimental, about their religion. She knew all the arguments, but like her most famous brother she discarded them. From her Aunt Harriet Foote, a high-church Episcopalian, she had learned at an early age some of the distinctions that were to disturb her for many years. Eventually she broke with her father's Calvinist church and became an Episcopalian, like her aunt.

At the age of twelve she could write learnedly on abstruse doctrines; and when not much older she could have easily explained the distinctions between supralapsarian, sublapsarian, and infralapsarian—because she had determined to be none of them. She knew Puritanism, that is, thoroughly, and she rejected it determinedly, denouncing "metaphysical analysis" and searching the Scriptures for gloriously beautiful and indistinct images (*RS,* 230). Her goal for people everywhere was a universal Christianity. "The Sermon on the Mount was, and still is," she wrote, "the most disturbing and revolutionary document in the world" (*RS,* 54). The hope of attaining this goal did not seem utopian. "He that believeth shall not make haste is the true motto of Christian reform" (*RS,* 56).

Yet for all this determination she was not attacking Calvinism, Puritanism, or her father; her separation from them was peaceful, tolerant, and incomplete. Except for the threat of everlasting hellfire, her views remained basically those of her father and her husband, her departure from their sternness being mostly a bodily shrinking from logical consequences. No matter how old she might grow, she would remain, in her soul, the same sweet, old-fashioned girl who had lisped her baby acquiescence. Her views were so bound by eighteenth-century

Calvinism that, labor as she would, she could never completely escape from her father's harsh emphasis on sin.

The Virgin Birth reassured her, and she envied Mary for having produced a child without male sexual cooperation. Jesus was entirely Mary's own, she explained in *Footsteps of the Master,* and she enjoyed a monopoly over him that no other mother has ever had (*RS,* 31–32). Lacking mortal father, Jesus was absolutely his mother's boy. As he himself was the union of the feminine and the divine, he had an understanding of women that other men cannot approach; and more-over, he is understood better by women, pure women, than by crude masculine creatures. "We can see no image by which to represent the Master," she concluded her cogitations, "but one of those loving, saintly mothers, who in leading along their little flock, follow nearest in the footsteps of Jesus" (*RS,* 78).

In this mood of exaltation she could hardly avoid another idea pleas-ant to her self-esteem: that through progressive revelations, Christian womanhood had, by the nineteenth century, reached an unparalleled height, attaining, as she wrote in *Woman in Sacred History,* "that pure ideal of a sacred woman springing from the bosom of the family, at once wife, mother, poetess, leader, inspirer, prophetess" (*WSH,* 28). And well it would be for the world, she could proceed, if this biblical model were honored more dutifully by wavering manhood.

The one serious question to disturb this view was Mary's modest retirement. "It is remarkable," said Stowe, hinting that it was also deplorable, "that Mary was never in any one instance associated in public work with Jesus." Thus she phrased one of the paradoxes of her own life: that she, who professed to believe in woman's domestic sphere, had been for years sticking her fingers into public pie and poking her stub nose into public business. There was only one explana-tion. "The delicacy of woman may cause her to shrink from the bustle of public triumph, but when truth and holiness are brought to public scorn she is there to defend, to suffer, to die" (*RS,* 39).

Personal disclosures like these are the most important part of Stowe's writings on religion, for they show how personal motives led to these lay sermons. Her religious experiences were a rich part of her life and the inspiration for several of her better novels, but the only doctrine that she derived from them was an absolute faith that Jesus saves those who love and serve him. Therefore she accepts the "clear-sighted love" of Fénelon, Francis de Sales (probably for his doctrinal writings), John Woolman, and the apostle John Eliot (*RS,* 120), and praises Virgil and

Socrates as gropers after truth (*RS,* 50–51); and finally she almost completely overcomes an ingrained childhood family prejudice. "The Protestant must not forbid the Romanist mission whose plain object seems to be to call sinners to repentence, and to lead professing Christians to a higher and holier life" (*RS,* 119).

The Christian Home

Harriet Beecher Stowe never suspected that a paradox of her simplified theology of heavenly love was her working hypothesis that money is good for body and soul. Calvin Stowe was less worldly than she, and yet however poor she felt herself to be she had always managed to hire servants for household work. In her relationship to publishers she was as definitely commercial as they were. Her calm assurance of self-righteousness knew none of the doubts of Jonathan Edwards or Lyman Beecher. About the purity of human nature she was as skeptical as they, with the single exception of the superior category to which she belonged: she was a Christian mother.

What might have been a revelatory book was the direct outgrowth of this assurance. Its title, briefly rendered as *The American Woman's Home,* bore the following additional explanation: "Principles of Domestic Science, being a guide to the formation and maintenance of economical, healthful, beautiful, and Christian Homes." It was published, under her name and Catherine's, in 1869; but other work prevented her from contributing much beyond her name.[4]

The American Woman's Home, since it is jointly attributed to Stowe, would no doubt be useful as a commentary on her thought; but the expression, alas, is not her own, and much of it is a revision of Catherine Beecher's many-versioned treatise on domestic economy. The exposition of the Christian family, of scientific domestic ventilation, of healthful drinks, doubtless met with Stowe's approval, and the chapter on the care of servants seems particularly in keeping with her ideas. The book was important in educating housewives in home management, but it was mainly important for Catherine, a recognized leader in a field where the distinction in title between married and unmarried women was still taken for granted.

Stowe's mature convictions on most of these subjects, unclouded by collaboration, are accessible in her other fiction and essays. From her serial novels and magazine articles can be retrieved, in scattered comments, the principles that might, under happier circumstances, have been organized into a major treatise. They will be found, virtually unaltered for tender intelligences, in stories for children, *Queer Little People* and *Little Pussy Willow*, reprinted from *Our Young Folks*.

For man and beast she invoked the same immutable morality. In the animal stories of *Queer Little People* (1867) virtue and vice remain human, whether in the homely sketches of family pets or in the allegories that make up the two halves of the volume. The morals of the allegories are standard: don't steal, proved by the story of a squirrel; don't yield to evil temptations, proved by the story of a robin that fell from its nest; don't be a meddler, proved by the story of a magpie. A narrative involving Miss Katydid and Miss Cricket is supposed to show the folly of drawing a color line. *Little Pussy Willow* (1870), a less harrowing *Pollyanna*, is an extended fable (123 pages) expounding the difference between the wholesome life of a country child and the pampered existence of a vain daughter of wealth. Stowe enriched the narrative, which is rather lame but overflowing with good counsel, with descriptions of bread making, interior decorating, and healthful clothing. She could appropriately have called her tale "The American Little Woman's Home."

For adult readers, more advice was generously introduced into thicker volumes. *My Wife and I* (1871) was a novel closely adapted to the needs and tastes of subscribers to the *Christian Union*, where it and a companion work, *We and Our Neighbors* (1875), were serialized.

Considering the amount and quality of the writing Stowe had published up to this time, readers find the stylistic imcompetency of *My Wife and I* surprising as well as painful. Stowe hardly needed to write down to any audience, however pious and humble; but the brutal truth is that she thoroughly approved of what she was doing, convinced that it must benefit the readers of the *Christian Union* and J. B. Ford's moral clientele. If this story were typical of literature in the America of 1871, no one could disagree with the thought of its opening sentence, that "the world is returning to its second childhood."[5]

Specifically, *My Wife and I* recounts the rise of the narrator, Harry Henderson, from poverty to affluence and happy mating with a daughter of wealth. The conscientious son of a New Hampshire minister, Harry, knowing he is unworthy of following his father's calling, devotes himself to serious journalism in New York, prospers, finds his Eva Van Arsdel—a sweet wholesome girl in spite of her worldly family—and sets up housekeeping.

It is odd how like an old lady this Harry Henderson is, odd how thoroughly his ideas are those of Mrs. H. B. Stowe. Don't smoke or drink, he warns his readers; don't take lightly the advice of elders; don't be worldly; don't marry for money; don't let college undermine your Christianity; don't neglect studying the Bible; don't become an aesthete, a reader of Rossetti or Swinburne; don't be vain about clothing; don't take a fashionable honeymoon trip; don't live in a rented house. To these principal commandments, others are added, of course, with painstakingly thorough development. Evidently the readers of the *Christian Union* or the young girls to whom the story was dedicated were in a parlous state of danger; but they undoubtedly could take advice.[6]

In brief, *My Wife and I* is a tract barely disguised as a serial story. An appeal for greater privileges for young women, it confuses that issue by its sarcastic portraits of two types of feminist leaders, a Mrs. Cerulian (also spelled Cerulean) and Miss Audacia Dangereyes, both based on types recognized in the contemporary feminists Elizabeth Cady Stanton and Victoria Woodhull. Stowe does less than justice to each, presenting her Audacia as a shameless hussy and Cerulian as a dupe. Exactly how much Stowe desired for young women is difficult to determine, as on the one hand she wanted the world run by mothers, and on the other didn't believe that women should have the vote.[7]

Her characters show the same confusion. The strong-minded girls have indistinct ambitions to do something with their lives, particularly to secure formal education, as in medicine, or to pursue other more vaguely described "professional studies." That is about as far as Stowe's plans went. She was greatly worried about the world, which was not virtuous, into which these newly educated women would be projected, and she did not know whether the finer clay of woman would overcome evil or succumb to its insidious influence. Humanity needs, says Harry Henderson for her, a loving and redeeming power by which it can be led back to virtue; but on the other hand, as his father-in-law points out, *good* women are not fit to govern the world, because they do not, and should not, know the rottenness of life.

No actual villain sullies her pages, no cheat or gross sinner except Audacia Dangereyes; but gloomy hints are cast about the utter worldliness and frivolity of all except the chosen few idealists. Rogues, sharpers, pickpockets, and bullies are so numerous that a woman's general rule of conduct must be to take for granted that every man will cheat if he can. Most horrible of all evils is that dirty, polluted literature by means of which, as Harry Henderson agrees, "we are fast drifting to destruction, it is a solemn fact" (134).

In *We and Our Neighbors; or, the Records of an Unfashionable Street,* Stowe fulfilled after four years a promise to continue the story of Harry and Eva Henderson's married life. So many loose ends were left dangling at the end of this second book that one judges the author had hopes, never fulfilled, of further extending the saga.

To the rules of conduct advanced in *My Wife and I* the sequel adds these: do not destroy faith in prayer; do not withdraw selfishly from life; do not marry in haste; do not parody hymns or concoct puns out of Holy Writ; do not ignore bodily hygiene; do not nag the servants; and do not use Gothic type on Christmas cards.[8]

The story itself, designed to show how to be happy, reveals more distinctly how easy it is to be unhappy. Marriage is its theme; and the one happy marriage in the book is that of Eva and Harry. In contrast, no fewer than six miserable women are paraded across the scene. These should be warning enough against matrimony, but Stowe blandly constructs her story around promoting marriages for two more of the Van Arsdel girls, Angelica and Alice.

To *We and Our Neighbors* has been reserved a distinction rarely bestowed upon Stowe's social novels, that of being reviewed at its appearance by a first-rate critic. Young Henry James, already embarked upon his career as literary craftsman, carefully examined the curious work, mystified by its formlessness and vulgarity. "It would be rather awkward to attempt to tell what Mrs. Stowe's novel is about," he confessed. The speech of the first families of New York, as he saw it reproduced by Stowe, struck him as a combination of rural Yankee dialect, Negro jargon, and paragraphs from the *Home Journal.* "None of Mrs. Stowe's ladies and gentlemen open their mouths without uttering some amazing vulgarism," he continued, content to remark that in addition to Eva, with her interest in *the humanitarian questions of the day,* "there are a great many other people, of whose identity we have no very confident impression, inasmuch as they never do anything but talk—and that chiefly about plumbing, carpetlaying, and other cognate topics" (New York *Nation* 21 [1875], 61).

Of a piece with these two novels is yet a third fictional effort to set society to rights. Though identified on the title page as a society novel, *Pink and White Tyranny* (1871) is also said, in the author's preface, "not to be a novel" but "a little commonplace history," "a story with a moral," a "sketch," and a "parable." The latter description is a true one, and the moral, put succinctly like the legend under a cartoon, is that no family should ever be led into divorce. "When once marriage is made and consummated, it should be as fixed a fact as the laws of nature," is the way Stowe phrases her proposition, even marriage to such a "shop-worn flirt" and "selfish, heartless little creature" as Lillie Ellis.[9]

Pink and White Tyranny is partly a warning against hasty marriages with strangers and partly a satire against the type of woman Lillie is: a selfish flirt who has lived the life of a petted creature, who likes French novels, who smokes cigarettes and lacks religious sense, who wants to serve wine at the dinner table, and who has no motherly instinct. But it was not Stowe's custom to let her story decide its own meaning. Having determined to attack divorce, she maintains that purpose, though the attack is by indirection and is likely to be entirely overlooked unless emphasized by special notes.

Throughout *Pink and White Tyranny* she is worried by the French influence on American Life. When John Seymour finds that his wife has been fibbing about her age, avowing only twenty years instead of the true twenty-seven, Stowe remarks that "a Frenchman would simply have smiled in amusement on the detection of the pretty feminine *ruse*" and that "only an Englishman or an American can understand the dreadful pain of that discovery to John *(PWT,* 95–96)."[10]

On the whole, poor little pink and white Lillie is a warning against French frivolity rather than the more horrible vices. "France, unfortunately, is becoming the great society-teacher of the world," our author generalizes, and inasmuch as "the Celtic races have a certain sympathy with deception," it is easy enough to see that if no just, generous, manly, religious young Anglo-Saxon fellow ever looked longingly upon such as she, he would never be tempted to divorce her. The moral ought to be that every "good solid chip of the old Anglo-Saxon block" should avoid young ladies who possess "the doubtful talent of reading French with facility" *(PWT,* 93, 96, 107, 204).[11]

Essays on Domestic Life

If as a social novelist Stowe was at her weakest, as a social essayist the change was more in manner than in matter. To express her ideas, which were on the whole more suitable to essay than story, she adopted for these pieces a style well recognized as acceptable to the better magazines, in which more editorial attention was given to the niceties of expression than in the churchly journals for which she contrived her fictional serials. Not as unforcedly cultured as that of George William Curtis or as frank as that of Ik. Marvel, her editorial associate on *Hearth and Home,* her essay style emphasized the same vivacity of manner that had opened to these writers, among other markets, *Putnam's Magazine* and the *Southern Literary Messenger.*

A congenial opportunity was afforded her in the articles, period pieces from the *Atlantic,* collected as *House and Home Papers* (1865), *Little Foxes* (1866), and *The Chimney-Corner* (1868). The type was well understood, the narrow limits of its satire recognized, and its underlying sentimentalism assumed. As Christopher Crowfield, a tolerant benevolent old body, she was given permission to write freely on any aspect of homemaking she desired. Taking for her motto, "No work of art can compare with a perfect home,"[12] she ranged far and wide, dispensing wisdom lavishly, restrained only by the conventions of the genre.

Remember the difference between a house and a home, she counseled her readers, anticipating the heap o' living hypothesis of a later authority. Don't try to have a stylish parlor, she warned them. The most beautiful furnishings are always the cheapest, she reminded them in one article, and was inspired to continue the subject in the following. She advised against too expensive a carpet, since by spending less on floor covering money might be saved for "engravings, chromolithographs, or photographs of some really *good* works of art."[13]

In the course of his monthly ramblings, Christopher Crowfield frequently returned to the subjects nearest Stowe's heart. On more than one occasion he came out unequivocally for women's suffrage—thus expressing one of Stowe's attitudes toward that puzzling proposal. He wrote caustically about French morals and manners; he showed a high regard for the manners and morals of New England. But of all the subjects connected with the home, his—or her, if you prefer—greatest attention, more than to religion, hygiene, entertainment, even furnishings, was centered on the servant problem, or, as he described it, "woman's natural, God-given employment of *domestic service.*"[14] The italics, which are hers, may be out of place for a liberated woman, but Stowe's liberation was unique, unlike that of other women of her time. In practice she was completely free from any control except her conscience. Her achievements had put her in the position of respect that feminists were striving to establish for all women. In her mind, however, she was doubtful of the relative value of the new proposals; she was skeptical of aggressive feminists to the same degree that she had been skeptical of extreme abolitionists.

Unlike the domestic novels of urban life, with their touches of grimy realism, the homey, housey articles for the *Atlantic* are relentlessly genial. Despite the references to Milton and Shakespeare, to Bacon, Pope, and Fénelon, to "old Plato" and "old Ben Jonson"—for Christopher was presumed to be a bookish man—they are dominated finally by familiar texts from "the dear old book of comfort." Their merit is a solid morality, for they are household sermons; and they must have pleased the author into thinking that they would do a great deal of good in reminding the dear *Atlantic* readers to avoid extravagance and folly in their homes.

If Stowe had spoken frankly for herself without ringing in Crowfield like a ventriloquist's dummy, her essays might have possessed at least autobiographical value; but the reader must always struggle to remember that in these three books she never speaks directly in character. The disguise is transparent; yet as obvious as it may be that Crowfield is not speaking, for the lady's desire to be a man could not endow her with masculinity, Stowe may not be speaking either.

All of these didactic writings, the fiction no less than the Crowfield essays, timely and fresh as they may have been when new, are now peculiarly empty. They were commercially valuable, as written for the magazines, putting money into the family coffers, which were generally low in spite of publishers' advances and queenly fees.[15] As books they were acceptable to the readers for whom they were intended, so that Stowe could afford to overlook the carping criticism of such organs of opinion as the *Nation*—in which Henry James's review of *We and Our Neighbors* appeared—just as she had been able to overlook the more strenuous criticism of her earlier novels in the days before the war.

Journalistic skirmishes seldom produced Stowe's best writing, important as they were to her livelihood. Between the bouts in her domestic fiction and essays with the troubled, unmanageable world in which she worked, she relived in other writing the vanished New England of her girlhood and her father's youth. In contrast to the sordid present, the New England past became in her writing an ideal era, a subject on which her quality as a writer was more adequately displayed. The four novels with New England settings that she wrote between 1858 and 1878 are attractive, atmospheric, and—except for the inexplicably powerful *Uncle Tom's Cabin*—her finest literary achievements.

Chapter Six

God's Countries

New England

In that very provincial expression of opinion, an elementary textbook on geography on which she permitted her name to appear as author in 1855, Stowe shows how completely New England was her center of the universe and the standard of moral excellence.[1] With the whole world to choose from, the first locality studied is New England; the first state mentioned, Connecticut; and the first college, Yale.

At the earliest opportunity, the story of the Pilgrims on the *Mayflower* is told, and the lesson to be drawn from it is repeated for the children of America. "The descendants of the Pilgrim Fathers in New England have been distinguished for their reverence for the Bible, for their good schools, and for their industrious habits. This is the reason why no people in the world have been more prosperous in every kind of business than those in New England; for God always makes those most prosperous who are most obedient to his laws in the Bible" (42).

The rest of the world has been created to set off New England's brilliance. Holland is a place "where the Pilgrim Fathers first went before they landed in New England"; the Quakers are admirable because they are "as careful as the New England people to have good schools"; and the westerners of the frontier draw virtues, such as they have, from Puritan forebears.

If region can be bred in the bone, two hundred years of New England Beechers had bequeathed to Stowe the spirit of the place. She had been brought up to have faith in New England, to see no virtues apart from it, and to regard it as the home of the latest chosen people. On these terms, given by nature, she could not fail. Just as among her first apprentice sketches the most successful are those about New England, so her later novels of New England have a liveliness unmatched elsewhere in her writings. But even so, the reader must not expect too much. Although she was one of the best-informed and most interesting interpreters of New England, Stowe was neither accurate nor complete, for disinterested objectivity was not part of her principles. Characteristically enough, she threw most of her stories out of perspective by dating them a few years before her birth, so that they occur in an idealized wonderland midway between her own experience and the visions of Cotton Mather.

A brief example of her selectivity is afforded by her sketch "The First Christmas in New England," as it appeared in the *Christian Union*. After describing the approach of *The Mayflower* to the Cape Cod country, she gives an imaginative account of how the holy day was spent. According to her, not only Christmas but the entire period was filled mainly with hymn singing, preaching, and pious conversations; the labor of constructing new homes and of protecting them from the dispossessed Indians was thrust into the background. Her Puritans are entirely too otherworldly to fit Governor Bradford's account of a Pilgrim Christmas. As he describes the day, it was spent, like all others, in godly labor, except for malingerers who were not adverse to shirking their responsibilities or fooling the authorities.

In Cotton Mather (1663–1728) Stowe found an old master best suited to the pattern of her conceptions. From her girlhood she loved him; his temperament, unfailingly pleasant to her, she described as that of "a delightful old New England grandmother," to which her own temperament reverberated gently and gratefully.[2] One need read very little of Mather's *Magnalia* or of his *Wonders of the Invisible World* before discovering the basis of her fondness, for Mather offers the same conception of the New England people as hers. They are, or at least were, the salt of the earth. "The world will do New England a great piece of Injustice, if it acknowledge not a measure of Religion, Loyalty, Honesty, and Industry, in the People there, beyond what is to be found with any other People for the Number of them. . . . New England was a true Utopia."[3]

Oldtown Folks (1869)

Stowe wrote four novels about New England life, in addition to a number of sketches, most of them collected in the *Mayflower* (1843) and in *Oldtown Fireside Stories* (1872). Her first volume, the same *Mayflower,* and her last, *Poganuc People* (1878), were New England to the core; her most important volume, *Oldtown Folks,* exhaled the very spirit of the region; and two other successful novels, *The Minister's Wooing* (1859) and *The Pearl of Orr's Island* (1862), owed their success largely to the flavor of New England in them. On these six books, in the last analysis, rather than on the gorgeous, unpredicted success of *Uncle Tom's Cabin,* Stowe's reputation as a writer must rest.

By far the most comprehensive of her New England novels, her own favorite among them, and indeed the best book she ever wrote is *Oldtown Folks,* in which she combined her husband's memories of his youth with her own dreams. Among all of her works, it is the book to be read with the maximum of quiet enjoyment and the minimum of exasperation. In it there is less obvious falsification than in her other works, and though it would not bear the test of rigorous formal analysis any more successfully than they, it is less tempting to the analytical-critical mind. By disarming criticism, *Oldtown Folks* turns attention from artistic improprieties to human relationships

The first six chapters of the book, almost one hundred pages, are in fact a model for creating a background for the story. Viewed entirely through the eyes of the narrator, Horace Holyoke as a boy, they become a leisurely guide to the village. With sociological detail the narrator recalls his childhood discovery, psychologically as well as geographically, of the group into which he was born. Many characters are introduced, some of whom become important in the narrative, others because they establish background and atmosphere.

That Horace's recollections create a too rosy picture of New England life at the end of the eighteenth century is undeniable, but the description, imaginatively convincing, is also at least historically plausible. Americans were an industrious, religious, prosperous people then, still tolerably unspoiled and modest. Within limitations, some Americans possessed the virtues that Amercians like to consider as belonging to them all without limitation. In its social setting, *Oldtown Folks* is the most realistic of Stowe's fiction; in the persuasiveness of its illusion, it is the most imaginative.

The action in these opening chapters is slight and straightforward. Told in the first person, the story relates the usual experiences of a boy's life in a small town. The unusual streak in his character, that he is a visionary lad (his visions duplicating Calvin Stowe's), is introduced later. In the beginning, having been left an orphan in early childhood, Horace is reared in his grandparents' family in the normal regimen of farming, churchgoing, and schooling. The last sentence of the sixth chapter foretells a change not entirely for the better. "But now that I have fairly introduced myself, the scene of my story, and many of the actors in it, I must take my readers off for a while, and relate a history that must at last blend with mine in one story" (*OF,* 84).

Ten chapters later Horace reappears as observer, with his visions, and meets the new characters, the orphan children Tina and Harry, strangers to the village manner and figures in a more complicated, unrealistic plot. Tina and Harry have been victims of maniacal sadists from whom they have escaped by a melodramatic ruse. Perhaps they do not spoil the book, since the story could not have continued without contrast and conflict, but they break the realism of the survey of Oldtown life. Throughout the remainder of the novel the contrived plot fits awkwardly into the reminiscent mood that is the best feature of the book.

The magnetic waif Tina is a character out of Stowe's other stories— the giddy girl, the little princess—and Stowe does not like her. She is beautiful and mentally uninteresting, the kind of woman who comes to a bad end or is rewarded beyond her deserts, depending more on the type of novel than on the character depicted. Stowe rewards Tina by marrying her to Horace, but she does so only after Tina's foolish marriage to Ellery Davenport, a Byronic intriguer and veritable Aaron Burr, an experience which has chastened her by a decade of suffering and humiliation. Though the colorful Tina is fictional, with no part in Calvin Stowe's life, except possibly in his dreams, she is the reason for introducing the Boston gentry into the story and thereby developing greater respect for the Oldtown people, only a three-hour carriage ride from the city but a whole age removed into idyllic pastoral life.

Whoever wants to learn from fiction what the immediate descendants of the Puritans were like before the coming of transcendentalism and the factory system need look no further than *Oldtown Folks*. They are shown—to some degree intentionally—in their self-will and self-righteousness, their hard-heartedness, their emotional starvation, and their simple snobbery. They are exhibited with their admixtures of bloodcurdling religion and practical charity and sympathy. The merriment of their life is revealed, as are their peaceful sleeping during the long Sunday wastes of sermon and prayers and the pranks of the children at church.

As finely colored as the descriptions of the country are, with beautiful yellow days leading into the harsh winter, they are excelled by Stowe's account of how the people lived during the administrations of President Washington and his immediate successors. As no tourist or visitor can, she takes a reader into their houses with their giant kitchen fireplaces and their musty parlors, and she shows them eating their beans and salt pork, taking their snuff, and drinking their cider. She initiates everyone into the mysteries of the weekend bath, the vigorous washings that used to make Saturday nights a terror to children of good families.

Nor was Stowe forgetful of the limitations of this life, desirable as she considered it to be. She liked the dominance given to the preacher in town, for he, the leading aristocrat, was followed by the other learned men; but she disliked the strong old-fashioned doctrine of President Jonathan Edwards and of Wigglesworth's *Day of Doom,* which she regarded as being monarchical and un-American. What pleased her most was the habit people had of arranging their views to suit their practices: the doctrines may have been hard, but the lives were merry.

Only one embarrassing feature of their beliefs does she skip over gingerly: their superstitions. Aside from the mild visions of Horace (in some of which Tina's mother comes and guides him) and the ghost that appears to old Crab Smith, there is absolute silence about the rich vein of popular lore that, having produced the witch hunts of previous generations, left its trail curling through the lives of all.

As in other literary collaborations, the partners are not always in agreement; sometimes the narrator sounds more like Calvin Stowe's wife than like Horace Holyoke. In the lectures on the proper education of children, the woman's voice is the louder. In the longer lectures on theology the speaker is not clear, since both collaborators were experts. Perhaps they never reached complete agreement, for chapter 29 begins with a warning that applies to other chapters as well. "Reader, this is to be a serious chapter, and I advise all those people who want to go through the world without giving five minutes' consecutive thought to any subject to skip it" (*OF,* 367). Although religion is the serious subject most discussed, and next to that a humane education for children, feminism and other matters receive attention. On many pages *Oldtown Folks* touches on subjects of more concern today than the differences in doctrine between Cotton Mather and Jonathan Edwards. Even Tina and her brother, young children, could be sorry for Crab Smith's wife, who had degenerated into a cowardly liar as the only escape from her years of marriage to a tyrannical husband.

The fifteen local color sketches in *Sam Lawson's Oldtown Fireside Stories* (1872), reprinted from the *Atlantic Monthly* and the *Christian Union,* are more closely connected with *Oldtown Folks* in name than in scope or weight. Sam had been introduced early in Stowe's novel as "the village do-nothing," the keen Yankee jack-of-all-trades whose particular delight is spinning yarns—in dialect. When Stowe had finished the

novel, she still had enough of Calvin Stowe's yarns on hand to fill a
volume. They are the stories—comic or serious, but always edifying—
Sam tells the boys, usually on their Saturday afternoon rambles. The
moral reflections, inserted with unremitting premeditation, differ from
those of *My Wife and I* principally in the dialect. "Lordy massy! riches
allers covers a multitude o'sins";[4] "There's a consid'able sight o' gump-
tion in grandmas" (*OFS*, 140); "Folks never does see nothing' when
they aint' lookin' where 'tis" (*OFS*, 153). Gentle satire is not completely lacking. "Folks allers preaches better on the vanity o' riches
when they's in tol'able easy circumstances" (*OFS*, 136). But no satire is
intended in passages like this: "Wal, ye see that 'are's the way fellers
allers begin the ways 'o sin, by turnin' their back on the Bible and the
advice o' pious parents" (*OFS*, 106–7).

The Final Word: *Poganuc People* (1878)

The true successor to Calvin Stowe's reminiscences is *Poganuc People;*
written about a decade later, it is a fictionalized account of Stowe's own
childhood. The Poganuc of the book is the uncontaminated Litchfield
"in the days when its people were of our own blood and race, and the
pauper population of Europe had not as yet been landed upon our
shores."[5] The minister is very like a benevolent Lyman Beecher, and
Dolly Cushman is even more like Hattie Beecher. So many changes
have been introduced, however, that only in spirit can the heroine be a
representation of Harriet, who did not, as Dolly does in the story,
marry a young man from Oxford University and settle down to the life
of a Boston matron. Another alteration makes Dolly the youngest of ten
children, but since the book is not a family chronicle, only two of the
older brothers have much to do with her, and their teasing is more
observable than their affection. Most of the story is personal, like the
scene that biographers love to reproduce: the ransacking of barrels of
theological tracts in the attic, followed by the discovery of the *Arabian
Nights,* appears here in full detail.

The story, which opens in a kitchen and ends in a cemetery, is
charmingly idyllic for its first two hundred pages. Two years are covered in these thirty-one chapters, with leisurely accounts of Christmas
customs (Presbyterian and Anglican), political elections, the Fourth of
July, church services, and lesser events like nutting in the open country-
side. The class organization of the village is clear, with the intellectual
leaders—parsons and judges—at its head, then the farmers and servants

(who speak in dialect), and a Negro or two. Of the three hired girls of the underpaid parson, the first is ideal and makes a good marriage within her class; the second is an insufferable whiner; and the third is an African woman, slow and disorderly but happy and humble.

Weary as the author of *Poganuc People* must have been by 1878, she created a convincing atmosphere in which the lectures and sermonettes have a natural place. A real human interest lies in the spirit of old days when people so like and so unlike Americans today muddled their curious ways through life. And those readers who regret the absence of art in the story should remember that for Stowe art was vanity; in her vocabulary, "work of art," as she reminded them, was nothing beyond "a hackneyed modern expression" (*PP*, 241).

To the analyst of Stowe's character, *Poganuc People* holds the special interest inherent in her memories of her father. Though she tried desperately to be just to him, she was unable to conceal her grievances. Thus, in the story, the reformation of Zeph Higgins, a self-willed, hard-hearted misfit, is not the direct result of the preacher's exhortations. When Mrs. Higgins died, she had beseeched Zeph to reconcile himself to the church; but the hardened sinner, though he attends, becomes increasingly certain that he is doomed to damnation. He is indeed a challenge to the church, but the preacher declines the struggle for his soul, saying that only God can speak to such a stubborn heart as Zeph's. God chooses to speak through Dolly, and old Zeph, reborn in grace through her, becomes Uncle Zeph, beloved by the whole town.[6]

Thus did Stowe, at the mature age of sixty-seven, declare the advantage of her religion of love over her father's religion of law; from early childhood, she asserted, she could have performed the Lord's work better than he. Such passages were the concluding skirmishes of her campaign against Jonathan Edwards, the great theological rival of her favorite, Cotton Mather, and the perpetual terror of her girlish religious gropings. On Edwards himself she had already wreaked what must have appealed to her as full, though tolerant, revenge. Two of her villains—in *Oldtown Folks* and *The Minister's Wooing*—are specifically described as Edwards's grandsons, the inevitable wicked fruits of false doctrines. Nor did her vengeance stop with these hints. "It was his power and his influence," she stated in *Oldtown Folks*, "which succeeded in completely upsetting New England . . . and casting out of the Church the children of the very saints and martyrs who had come to this country for no other reason than to found a church" (*OF*, 364).

To invective against Edwards she added the device of reductio ad absurdum in the person of a follower who, ruthlessly torturing his congregation with the sense of their unmitigated depravity, was privately "an artless, simple-hearted, gentle-mannered man" who "wore two holes in the floor opposite his table in the spot where year after year his feet were placed in study" (*OF,* 380) Thus she worked out the complete justification for rejecting her father's views: the saints had been driven from the church in which the only escape from horrible doctrines was refusing to believe them.

This mellow understanding is the very essence of those portions of *Poganuc People* in which, on more than one occasion, Stowe permits herself innocent quips at Lyman Beecher's expense. In one place, after the minister has been discussing free will and divine agency with a puzzled parishioner and settling the matter to his own satisfaction, she comments, "Having thus wound up the sun and moon, and arranged the courses of the stars in the celestial regions, the Doctor was as alert and light-hearted as any boy, in his preparations for the day's enterprise" (*PP,* 223). Another incident related his strategic use of a quotation against Christmas ceremonies, taken from the second century Clemens Alexandrinus. His daughter comments that although few in the congregation would have appreciated who Clemens was, all of them admired their minister as a learned man "and were triumphant at this new proof of it." His absentmindedness becomes, in another facetious description, "a little habit of departing unceremoniously into some celestial region of thought in the midst of conversation." It was, to be sure, a pardonable weakness; but this similar inability to enter into the life of his young daughter, though also pardonable, never ceased to arouse her resentment. She found herself apologizing for him, for two reasons: he had never been a mother, and he had never understood true Christianity.

The last few chapters of the book are a hurried effort to bring the story to a conventional satisfactory close. Suddenly Dolly is a fine young lady ready for love and marriage. As she is no longer the child Hattie Beecher, and as Stowe the writer never cared much for stories of premarital love, the narrative is perfunctory.[7]

Two Other New England Novels

Of Stowe's two other New England stories, first published as serials in the *Atlantic Monthly* and the *Independent,* the minor work *The Pearl of Orr's Island* (1862) is now the more agreeable reading. In its day, however, *The*

Minister's Wooing (1859) was more famous. It had the publicity advantages of James Russell Lowell's editorial endorsement, of subsequent controversy over historical and doctrinal accuracy, and of the use of the Beecher archives, to which family biographers have referred. Such circumstances have given the book undue prominence, especially since its intrinsic merits as a chronicle of New England have been more fully revealed in its successor by a dozen years, *Oldtown Folks*.

The Pearl of Orr's Island stands apart from Stowe's other stories, since in it for the only time in her works she exploited the achievements of the New England sailors. The opening pages, in fact, are unusually charming, and Sarah Orne Jewett spoke admiringly of them in an autobiographical preface to *Deephaven*, expressing deep gratitude for the book's revelation to her, a young girl, of "those who dwelt along the wooded seacoast and by the decaying, shipless harbors" of her native state. To a degree, this charm persists, but only to a degree, for the development of the story does not fulfill the high promise of the start. As Jewett wrote on another occasion, in a letter to Annie Fields, "Alas, that she couldn't finish it in the same noble key of simplicity and harmony."[8]

Basically, the plot of *The Pearl of Orr's Island* is no more complicated than most of Stowe's ingenuous fables: the love of a gentle, matronly child for a headstrong, wild youth concludes with the death of the girl and the spiritual awakening of the young man. The complications are the youth's struggle with his pride and the thoughtless rivalry of a flirting neighbor girl; but the native nobility of all three is sufficient guarantee of the happy solution. For is not death a happy solution? Stowe asks, using the demise of the saintly Mara as an opportunity to expound the true Christian attitude toward death. Other inescapable asides concern spiritualism, the divine inspiration of the Bible, and, at length, the proper education of children.[9]

This last problem is more intimately connected with the story than might be suspected, for Moses, the young hero, is, if the truth be told, a problem child. Not only is he a waif and an orphan, washed up on the Maine coast by a storm; but he is the son of parents who were rich, Catholic, southern, and, in part, Spanish—a combination of handicaps for which the only hope is rigorous education in a New England sea captain's God-fearing family. The task requires all the force of Mara's motherly love (developed in her before she was thirteen) and all the "innocent hypocrisy" and "gentle vindictiveness" that Stowe specifies as two saintly and womanly virtues (*POI*, 229, 246).

To make the treatment stick, the emphasis of Mara's death is required; and so Stowe leaves Moses, master of his own ship, a neophyte
in prayer, and the husband of the little flirt next door, now also
chastened and sobered into nobility. The moral is clear: the American
chosen people, with their harsh visages but tender hearts, were able as a
group to mold the "real wild ass's colt" into a presentable imitation of a
little Beecher Calvinist.

A simple tale? *The Minister's Wooing,* except for the more important
character involved, is hardly less simple in plot: a conventional situation, the love of three men for a girl, is resolved without surprises. Of
the heroine, Mary Scudder, a small-town jewel, it need but be said
that, like Mara, she is a model of Christian girlhood and the nearest
approach to an angel to be found on this earth. The desirous males
include Dr. Samuel Hopkins, a divine well known in his day; Colonel
Aaron Burr, well known in this era; and young James, a lad entirely
fictional, the lucky suitor. Thus there are really three wooings in the
story, and the outcome is not difficult to foresee.

Objected to by the girl's mother, James goes to sea and is apparently
drowned in a shipwreck, with his salvation in doubt because of his
incomplete acceptance of Christianity. Colonel Burr, arriving in town
on a visit, can not resist the temptation to flirt with gentle Mary. The
Puritan maiden—Stowe is fond of applying the adjective to eighteenth-
century New Englanders—finally gives him an edifying lecture and,
simultaneously, his walking papers, thus leaving the way clear for the
minister.

Doctor Hopkins is a fairly concrete character. Stowe, who knew
preachers from *a* to *z,* introduced into her portrait a large share of her
father's theology and a number of her husband's character traits. The
learned, good man—utterly without imagination or what is commonly
understood as romance—lives in the world of high idealism and biblical citation. His wooing proper consists in asking Mary's mother, who
would be a much better match for him, whether the girl will accept
him. When the offer is brought to Mary, she has no need to feign
surprise. Resigned to God's will, after suffering over her sweetheart's
supposed death, she resolves to marry the minister to gratify her
mother and him. "When we renounce self in anything," she confides to
James's mother, anticipating Christopher Crowfield, "we have reason
to hope for God's blessings; and so I feel assured of a peaceful life in the
course I have taken."[10]

With no higher hopes than these, she is rudely upset by the return of

James, full of love, Christian now because of his parting conversations with her, and incidentally rich. Duty, of course, is to carry her through marriage with the minister; but Miss Prissy Diamond, the village dressmaker and know-it-all, taking matters into her own hands, reveals to the good minister where his fiancée's heart lies, and the necessary sacrifice becomes his instead of Mary's.

James and Mary are united. "The fair poetic maiden, the seeress, the saint, has passed into that appointed shrine for woman, more holy than cloister, more saintly and pure than church or altar—a *Christian home.*"[11] Eventually, a sentence informs the readers, good Doctor Hopkins marries a "woman of fair countenance" who presents him with sons and daughters.

A typical product of Stowe's mind, *The Minister's Wooing* inevitably repeats many of her ideas. She regarded any good woman as a better evangelist than the greatest divine; and the scene in which Colonel Aaron Burr, listening to a lecture on his sins delivered by Mary, breaks down and weeps is doubly unbelievable in its simplicity (*MW, 478*).

The minister whose futile, undignified courtship was thus circumstantially disclosed was the historic and celebrated Dr. Samuel Hopkins, whose biography had been written shortly before by Dr. Park, president of the seminary at Andover in which Dr. Stowe was teaching. Disturbed by the geographical and biographical inaccuracies in her story as it appeared serially in the *Atlantic,* Park urged the author to correct her errors before allowing publication in book form, a well-meant suggestion that she refused to consider; Stowe had a fine scorn for mere literal accuracy.[12]

In comparison with *Oldtown Folks, The Minister's Wooing* suffers from thinness of detail; and yet, since the book appeared earlier, when *Oldtown Folks* followed it was inevitably criticized adversely for its similarities to its forerunner. Thus Florine McCray, Stowe's unauthorized biographer, complained of "a poverty of invention" in *Oldtown Folks,* specifying, in addition to repetitions within the book itself, the reincarnation of Stowe's typical minister (attributed by McCray to Lyman Beecher) and her typical schoolmaster (John P. Brace) under the thin disguise of new names. McCray also regretted the reappearance of Mrs. Marvyn as Esther Avery and the awkward entrance of "a cousin" of Aaron Burr to imitate that gentleman's fascinating villainies. Such objections, well founded as they are, need never bother the reader who takes a friendly hint to postpone indefinitely his reading of *The Minister's Wooing* in favor of a glance at *Oldtown Folks.*[13]

Italy Fails the Test

Italy, which had fascinated and thrilled Stowe on her third memorable European vacation, fell far short of her ideal of Christian propriety. As might be expected from her family prejudices, she was near her weakest in *Agnes of Sorrento* (1862), her Italian romance. Exotic Italy, which tested the penetration of Hawthorne in *The Marble Faun* and the political acumen of James Fenimore Cooper in *The Bravo*, hurled her to ignominious defeat. With no great cause to inspire her and no inbred traditions to lend body to her work, she had little left but romantic tricks and a limitless supply of prejudices. *Agnes of Sorrento* is therefore one of the most personal of her works, and one of the most provincial. It is more restrictedly New England than *Oldtown Folks;* and in its lack of historical perspective it is anything other than what its title page professes: "an historical novel of the time of Savonarola."[14]

The book, though originating in the delight Stowe felt in Italy, is filled with her inbred deprecation of Catholic customs and doctrines, and even of Italy itself. "Our enlightened Protestantism" enabled her to be charitable (*AS*, 150–51). "Let us not, from the height of our day with the better appliances which a universal press gives us, sneer at the homely rounds of the ladder by which the first multitudes of the Lord's flock climbed heavenward" (*AS*, 112).

Consequently, she never sneered; she was content to patronize. She sorrowed at the thought of "these good women," the Catholic sisters, "unwittingly deprived of any power of making comparisons, or ever having Christ's sweetest parable of the heavenly kingdom enacted in homes of their own" (*AS*, 34). She relegated to its proper place "a picture of the Crucifixion by Fra Angelico; which, whatever might be its *naive* defects of drawing and perspective, had an intense earnestness of feeling" (*AS*, 291).[15] The piety and the sincerity of this artist she found, undoubtedly, more worthy of note for their relative absence throughout the greater part of Italian life. "In fact," she generalized, "the climate of Southern Italy and its gorgeous scenery are more favorable to voluptuous ecstacy than to the severe and grave warfare of the true Christian soldier" (*AS*, 186). And the uppers of the boot, she suspected, were of no better material than the toe.

The story takes its name from the heroine, the beautiful young Agnes, whom everyone loved—as was the case of Eva St. Clare—and who was favored or afflicted, like Tina or Mary Scudder, by three particular adorers. One, the candidate advanced by her grandmother

Elsie, is a simple clod named Antonio—but there are no peasants in New England; the second, her father confessor Francesco—contrast the poor soul with Dr. Hopkins—is driven nigh to insanity by his guilty passion; and the third, the young cavalier Prince Agostino Sarelli, is eventually the lucky man. The love story, a mere excuse, was as usual far removed from the author's main interest; for, since the morality of the Catholic church fascinated her, she found herself writing a tract.

Her technique in picturing the Italian past was the same as that she had used in discussing slavery: with no concern for traditions or facts, she asked herself what the possible types of misconduct were; and she was sure that, if they could exist, they did. From this consideration she built what she thought was a truthful image of the society at its worst. For the other side of the picture she assumed that, as far as permitted by human frailty, the ideals of the institution were occasionally achieved. From this contrast of opposites she derived a story that was strongly melodramatic and should have been, in this instance, much more exciting than it turned out to be.

Defective imagination rather that defective thinking made *Agnes of Sorrento* commonplace. Consistent with her habit, Stowe introduced young Agostino, a dissolute Byronist like Ellery Davenport and Aaron Burr, who sought to seduce Agnes by flattery and jewelry; but Stowe thought better of him by the ninth chapter and altered his past to transform him into a victim of oppression. Finally reconciling herself to him, in spite of his Italian blood, she made him as one with herself: his "blind sense of personal injury" had been converted into a "fixed principle of moral indignation and opposition" (*AS*, 349). Equally confusing is the character of Il Padre Francesco, who is unconsistently enlightened and superstitious, progressive and reactionary.

Stowe was on the whole rather too casual with her characters. She did not follow them as closely as trained readers demand. She said about one of them, Antonio as it happened, "We may have introduced him to the reader before, who likely enough has forgotten by this time our portraiture; so we shall say again . . . " (*AS*, 227). Evidently she herself was not sure whether she had mentioned Antonio; the matter was of slight importance to her, and she obviously expected her readers to have no greater interest in him than she had. She never decided upon the status of her hero; she describes him as penniless and without influence but almost simultaneously refers to his wealthy and powerful relatives. The women fare somewhat better. The heroine Agnes is consistently made the mouthpiece of the author's religion of love, and two older women are allowed to utter many homely truths in the manner of New England crones freely speaking their minds.[16]

Florida

It is indeed pleasantly restful to turn from this misconceived Italian romance to the humbler pages of *Palmetto-Leaves* (1873), a book of sketches about Florida that shows a more successful escape. In Mandarin, a very small town on the St. Johns River near Jacksonville, where Stowe had settled in the late 1860s, she found the joy of a foreign country without the bewilderment of violent change. She stated her primary purpose in moving south (aside from her son's health) as a desire to improve the Negroes by providing education and Episcopalianism for their "immature minds." That kind soul, her husband, held services for both white and black folks; but as she was kept busy with her writing, her own charities were more likely to be on behalf of organizations or of individuals who could be reached by mail. She was highly pleased by the piety and industry of the Negroes around her, seeing them "very happy in their lowly lot" and—pleasing her equally—"growing richer and richer."[17]

But all such benevolent reform became, as time passed, incidental. In her deep, almost pathetic attachment to the calm South, her joy in her Florida winter home was produced less by any help she might give than by that she was unquestionably receiving. Primarily, she was happy in a new way because she was being withdrawn from the troubles of active life. "The world that hates Christ" was eliminated in Mandarin, her "calm isle of Patmos" (AF, 343). There she could write her three hours a day when she was able, or spend a winter reading lives of Christ and thanking God she was one of the elect.

Upon occasion she withdrew voluntarily from this haven of rest, for example, for a speaking tour in the fall and winter of 1872–73; and she was drawn unwillingly from it at other times, for instance, by the charge of adultery brought against her brother by his young friend, Theodore Tilton, in 1874. Though her faith in Henry Ward never wavered, the strain of the protracted trial and the distasteful notoriety accompanying it damaged her health, perhaps permanently. To her mind, the proceedings against Henry Ward were a clear case of the world against Christ. Her faith in him remained unshaken, but legal expenses of $118,000 were a form of the Lord's chastening that she had never courted.[18]

Only slightly less personal than her letters from these years are the sketches for the *Christian Union* published in 1873 as *Palmetto-Leaves*. They show how within half a decade she had adapted herself to the physical life of the Old South, and how remarkably she had identified her interests with those of Florida. "Your Northern snowstorms . . . hold back our springs" was one of her complaints against her erstwhile fellow Yanks; and she shuddered at an invitation to revisit Cincinnati. The accusation that the state of Florida consisted of nine-tenths water and one-tenth swamp deeply hurt her. The malarial fevers, she responded, were mild compared with those of New York and New England; and for the deadly moccasin snake she found no stronger adjective than "unsavory."[19]

She liked almost everything in Florida, and a perpetual song of joy fills the pages of the book. Like a missionary in the field, Stowe sent her glowing reports north. Incidentally, she was collecting money for her private charity, the church and school at Mandarin; but she was filled with zeal for the whole Jacksonville-St. Johns River region. Practical woman that she was, she answered questions about the price of board at the winter resorts—it ranged from eight to thirty-five dollars a week—and about the price of land—there was good land at from one to five dollars an acre. She gave definite instructions about clothes, summarized the techniques of producing oranges and preserving figs, and described the flora of the region in copious detail. Above all, though, it was the glorious climate that she expatiated upon, eloquently testifying to its value for the aged as well as for invalids and children.

In adjusting herself to this new life, she showed greater power of adaptation than could have been suspected in an old Yankee. She learned not to expect all of the exactitude of New England; she patiently took cognizance of what could or could not be demanded. Hard experience taught her the difference between a Negress brought up in the fields and one educated as a house servant; and, instead of complaining that Negroes were lazy, she was amazed at the work they could accomplish under a hot sun that would have been, so she thought, a white man's death. She regarded them as already the best labor in the South, and, when *carefully looked over* (she italicized the phrase), as productive as any laborers that could be hired in the North and more obedient and more easily satisfied (*PL,* 315). The reconstructed state of Florida, as she saw it, was a nearer approach to God's country than New England, outside of Cotton Mather's pages, had ever revealed itself to be.

The people of Florida liked her and Calvin Stowe as well as she liked them. To be sure, there were occasional impoliteness and insult to be borne, such as persons refusing to remain in church with the Stowes; but these were more than outweighed by formal receptions in her honor and by the obvious gratitude felt toward both Stowe and her husband. As the local history of Mandarin shows, she was the small town's leading citizen and is still its principal claim to attention. To some of her neighbors she was only a kindly lady with a dimly famous name— the era of *Uncle Tom's Cabin* was so far in the past—and the literate ones accepted her as if she were a convert eager to repair through good works the damage she had done in the past.

Palmetto-Leaves and her magazine articles—the best publicity imaginable, unsolicited, free, and palpably sincere—were strong arguments in her favor. The writings not only brought tourists but the author herself was a tourist attraction. Stereoscopic views of the Stowes on their veranda and on the spacious lawn in front of their home were sold nationally. A navigation company, which instituted round-trip excursions up the St. Johns River from Jacksonville to Mandarin, guaranteed a view of the Stowe orange grove and optimistically hinted at opportunities to see the celebrities also. Though the tourists were sometimes a nuisance to the Stowes, they were an asset to the community.[20]

Whatever Stowe may have intended to do for education and religion in Florida when she settled there, it is clear that she reaped the benefits of her move in improved health and peace. She had discovered that the South, if properly colonized by Episcopalians, could be kept as free from debauchery and debasing vice as the North; and the South offered an added inducement to true godliness: the mild and tolerant climate. Increasing age, unfortunately, and decreasing mental activity obscured this true moral of geography. Her immigration into God's country of the soul had been too long delayed by frantic diggings into the stony wastes of New England. Quite idyllic, however one looks at it, was her escape from New England, the domain of a justly stern and angry God, into the mildness of Florida, the creation of love and pity. In spite of her distrust of the world, the universe had accepted her: the South was the triumph of her life, the accidental fulfillment of her dreams.

Chapter Seven
Magazinist

In Harriet Beecher Stowe's youth, magazines had been her only market as well as her first teacher. In her maturity they remained her most regular outlet and her most dependable public. Hence magazines, for her more than for most writers, are primary sources of study. Since much of what she wrote for them never reached book publication, their significance is inescapable. Equally important, her routine writing for magazines shows the continuity of her literary career.

After the success of *Uncle Tom's Cabin* Stowe continued producing single articles or short series for miscellaneous publications, but she concentrated on a few favorites with which she established formal relationships as a featured contributor. Three of these, each informative on this aspect of her work, are the *Independent, Hearth and Home,* and the *Christian Union.*

The *Independent*

In 1852, when Stowe joined the staff, the *Independent* was a four-page weekly newspaper or magazine like the *Evangelist,* in policy as well as appearance. The *Independent* described itself as "conducted by pastors of Congregational churches," with Leonard Bacon, Joseph P. Thomson, and Joshua Leavitt as editors, and Henry Ward Beecher (liberal) and George B. Cheever (conservative) as signed contributors. On 1 July 1852, Stowe was listed as a third special correspondent, a position she held for ten years. During the remainder of 1852 and 1853, she sent the *Independent* nothing essential, only the story "How to Make Friends with Mammon" (later reprinted in *The May Flower* of 1855), some verse, letters on the Stowe-Parker libel controversy, and chapters from the *Key to "Uncle Tom's Cabin,"* printed in advance of the book. During this period, the magazine carried many stories about her and the progress of *Uncle Tom's Cabin,* but for over a year, including the whole of 1853, she sent nothing, although her name was carried as a contributor.

In 1854—the paper had meantime expanded to eight pages—she was more active. One of her pieces was "An Appeal to the Women of the Free States," a persuasive plea that they work for the abolition of slavery. The others were ten articles in a series called "Shadows on the Hebrew Mountains," lay sermons on piety, faith, and resignation, with such morals as "give up the temptations of the world" and "afflictions are for man's good—but not necessarily good in themselves." The "Shadows," which have never been reprinted, are in the style that she had already begun in the *Evangelist* and that she later displayed fully in *Footsteps of the Master.*

Throughout 1855, only one of her seven articles had much to say. Called "Books," it was a mild commercial plug for the *Plymouth Hymn-Book,* edited by Henry Ward Beecher, a few hundred words of general praise, to accompany the publication of the book. Other contributions were innocuous observations on weather and gardening, birds, flowers, and weeds.

In the following year, 1856, she sent "Our Friends in Heaven," "Mothers of the Men in Kansas," and "Anti-Slavery Literature." In this last article she reviewed some publications of the Anti-Slavery Society, including books by William C. Nell and Charles G. Parsons for which she also wrote introductions. The comments, here, as in the introductions, are rather thin. "A few years ago there was no anti-slavery literature," she said—meaning that for her there was none.[1] This review also speaks favorably, in the manner of a commercial announcement, of antislavery fiction: she was hard at work on *Dred.*

During 1857 she sent four "Letters from Europe" in the general vein of the earlier *Sunny Memories of Foreign Lands,* one dated from Rome, the other three from Paris. In 1858 there was more verse, some stories like "Our Charley," reprinted in the *Writings,* four unreprinted essays in defense of revivals, one against the Jesuits, one calling attention to the achievements of Negroes, and an appeal to the churches to come out strongly against slavery. These have more force and vitality than most of her writings for the *Independent,* and they furnish a cross section of her interests at the time.

The spring of 1859 finds only two articles on "The Higher Christian Life," but in December of that year she began a series of letters from Europe. Twenty-three in all, they ran from 1 December 1859 to 23 August 1860. They are fully equal to *Sunny Memories,* and it is probable that they would have been worked over into a book, had not the Civil War kept the interests of the readers nearer home. The material of these letters is the basis for Stowe's later inferior series for the New York *Ledger,* 1865.

On her return to America, Stowe sent the *Independent* six more articles during 1860, including a friendly note on the visit of British royalty, one of her now rare moral tales, two more articles urging the churches to take a stronger stand, an attack on President Buchanan, and an editorial rejoicing in Lincoln's election: "We are aware that the Republican Party are far from being up to the full measure of what *ought* to be thought and felt on the slavery question. But they are for *stopping the evil*—and in this case to arrest is to cure. . . . Meanwhile, the friends of anti-slavery principle should not relax labor."[2]

In 1861 Stowe began her serial story *The Pearl of Orr's Island*, suspended after seventeen chapters and resumed only after a lapse of seven months.[3] For shorter articles, requiring less concentration, she wrote "Getting Ready for a Gale," one week after Fort Sumter had been bombarded, several denunciations of her old enemy the London *Times*, and defenses of the goodwill of the English people. The following year she wound up her connection with the *Independent* in a series of six articles combining biblical stories with an appeal for immediate emancipation of the Negroes. Throughout them she necessarily took issue with President Lincoln over his desire to save the Union at whatever cost. The abolition of slavery, she kept insisting, was the first duty of a Christian commonwealth.

Stowe's association with the *Independent*, during the decade between 1852 and 1862, was not especially propitious, although it did produce, in some of her travel letters and later political editorials, articles that deserved inclusion in her collected *Writings*. Too often she wrote as if fumbling for a subject, probably because her main interests lay with *Dred, The Minister's Wooing, Agnes of Sorrento*, or other writing she was doing outside the paper. Fate was against her too, for during such crises as the Dred Scott excitement and John Brown's raid, she was in Europe, unable to express quickly enough the indignation that she felt.

The suspension of her serial story marred her relationship with the *Independent*. In announcing her inability to continue on 4 April 1861, she came the nearest to a direct falsehood in her career, for she gave as her reason the necessity of revisiting Maine for further observation "to give the story the finish and completeness I wish." For this white lie she made full atonement in "A Card" of 21 November 1861, announcing the resumption of the story in the following issue. Here she again fibbed a bit in asking, "Who could write on stories, that had a son to send to battle?" Finally, however, she gave the true reason—overwork.

One special service that the *Independent* performed for Stowe was to act as her press agent. Her name on its front page week after week, whether she was writing for the issue or not, had the effect of reiterated advertisement; and beyond this the magazine generously reviewed her books. When *The Minister's Wooing* was attacked, the *Independent* ran an editorial, "Theology and Morality in *The Minister's Wooing*," denying that she had gone over to Unitarianism. On the same page it printed another article on the same subject, and on another page a letter from a correspondent (9 February 1860). Nowadays one would assume logrolling, but Stowe's circle never suspected themselves guilty of such a practice.

Hearth and Home

When the weekly domestic magazine *Hearth and Home* was established, beginning with the issue of 26 December 1868, the editors were Donald G. Mitchell and Harriet Beecher Stowe. This was the first and the last time in her career that Stowe took public responsibility for preparing a magazine regularly. Her duties were slighter than her title of associate editor suggested, for they were limited to supplying a weekly column, with Mitchell shouldering the main labors. Even this routine work was beyond her, for her last column appeared on 30 October 1869, and her name disappeared from the editorial acknowledgments on 20 November 1869. The strain of regular weekly assignments was too much for her, although she cannot be accused of laziness, since in the years 1868–69 four of her books were published—*The Chimney-Corner, Men of Our Times, Oldtown Folks,* and *The American Woman's Home.*

In their skipping from topic to topic, and in their occasional emptiness, the contributions themselves show what her difficulties were. Since none of her forty papers for *Hearth and Home* has been reprinted, a glance at them, in their original order, is a rewarding glimpse into her workshop.

The first issue contained her "Greeting," one of her clearest statements on the position of women. With the liberals she maintained that women should have the right to vote, to engage in business, and to make themselves useful as they wished; but with the conservatives she maintained also that the rights of voting and trading were far inferior to woman's greatest vocation, that of wife and mother. Thus she offered a benevolent, if distant, encouragement to the movement for feminine freedom, while leaving herself free to oppose any particular step taken on its behalf. For her second offering she retreated to "Rights of Dumb Animals."

The following week she began a series of articles on commercial writing, a topic that lasted four weeks, giving way, 6 February 1869, to "How to Treat Babies." The next piece was a filler, answers to correspondence received through the magazine. She followed this with praise of some beautiful chromolithographs. Then she took a week's vacation.

In March she discussed, week by week, gardening, commercial writing again, how to buy a carpet—as in Christopher Crowfield's "The Ravages of a Carpet"—and how to beautify living rooms with flower pots made from old tin cans. For the month of April her column was acceptably filled by travel letters from Florida. These are in the spirit of the later book, *Palmetto-Leaves,* her never-ending enthusiasm establishing her talent as a publicity agent. The May articles were also entirely on her travels, which were summed up in her first two June articles, "From the St. Johns, South, to the St. Johns, North" and "Homeward to Canada."

For the last weeks of June she discussed, in two installments, "What Shall Young Girls Read?" In the first of these she recommended the *Pictorial History of England* and *Ivanhoe.* The second went on to *The Talisman,* Strickland's *Queens of England,* and the histories of Froude and Macaulay. On 3 July she printed a sympathetic and informative article on "The Colored Labor of the South," an evaluation of progress since emancipation. After this she took another week's leave, and followed it on 17 July with a pointless discussion of "Country and City."

Beginning on 24 July 1869, the magazine provided her with illustrated covers depicting, week by week, "Four Scenes in the Life of a Country Boy," choice period pieces on which she commented appropriately. The titles, "Leaving Home," "The Temptation and the Fall," "Further On," and "At Last," practically tell the story. The pitiful yokel, having become a forger, is led off to prison by a detective—the climax of a series of scenes not quite in the spirit of Hogarth.

On 21 August 1869 she discussed "The Handy Man" around the house, and the following week returned, more vitally, to women's rights, in "What Is and What Is Not the Point in the Woman Question." In a word, the point is money; and justice still holds, as in revolutionary days, that taxation without representation is tyranny. Another week's leave of absence followed.

September found the associate editor on her travels again, with four articles inspired by various places in New England. On 9 October she changed the subject to ask, "Who Earned That Money?" answering that the wife, by saving, was also a true earner. The article for 16 October 1869 considered "Our Early Rose Potatoes," and that of 30 October, called simply "Hartford," told the world that she was home.

Once home, she lacked either ambition or energy to continue further with *Hearth and Home.* The Byron controversy was already upon her, and she was saving her energies for the publication, in the years 1870–71, of *Lady Byron Vindicated, Little Pussy Willow, My Wife and I,* and *Pink and White Tyranny.*

Stowe's associate editorship of *Hearth and Home,* though merely an episode in her busy life, shows her difficulties in finding vital subjects for weekly discourses. She had the habit of repeating herself and the equally fatal one of using up her good leads too fast. When in doubt, she fell back on her old standbys, except that straight religious discourse was not permitted in *Hearth and Home.* Travel became her greatest source of copy: fourteen of her forty articles are about travel, eight of them concerning Florida. Six of the others are on homemaking problems (the special field covered by the magazine), three on feminism, one on kindness to animals, and eight on miscellaneous subjects. The only new vein uncovered is a group of seven articles on writing and reading, a significant addition to her meager comments on these subjects in her letters and the collected *Writings.*

In her manner of writing there are no distinctions between the *Hearth and Home* articles and the earlier ones for the *Independent* or the later ones for the *Christian Union.* They are hasty sketches, far removed from the more carefully edited longer essays for the *Atlantic Monthly.* Stowe left *Hearth and Home* for several reasons: better prospects elsewhere, overwork, and the fact that the magazine owed her five thousand dollars (*FW,* 544).

The *Christian Union*

Of all the journalistic connections of the Beechers, the *Christian Union* was probably the happiest personally. This magazine—which later developed into the *Outlook,* enjoying a long and successful existence— was published by the firm of John Bruce Ford and Company, the principal publisher of Stowe's later books.

The firm itself was established out of love for Henry Ward Beecher.

Both Ford and his younger partner, John Raymond Howard, who has told the story in his *Remembrance of Things Past,*[4] were idolizers at the Beecher shrine, and the firm was founded to exploit their idol's talents. All was optimism around Ford and Company's offices, for the firm was prosperous from the start, and when the *Christian Union* was finally reorganized in 1870, with Beecher himself as editor, its pages breathed a calm assurance that all was well with the world. Failure was to come almost as suddenly, a few years later, with Beecher's spectacular fall from public favor, but meanwhile there was a profitable subscription list of over two hundred thousand names.[5]

In his "Salutory" for the new magazine, dated 1 January 1870, Beecher explained the title and policy of the paper. It was to be a family journal, that is, of general, not specifically religious, interest, but none the less "distinctly Christian influence." It was to be devoted to "oneness of Christian sympathy," though not to "oneness of Church . . . that phantom, a Universal Corporate Unity of Christians." Beecher was determined to avoid all doctrinal controversy in an attempt to shed his own views on as wide a segment of the magazine buying public as possible. He worked energetically on the *Christian Union,* supplying weekly chats and editorials as well as his sermons, and even during the days of the Tilton adultery trial he kept a brave face in talking of himself and his troubles.

In the second issue he began introducing the members of his family to the magazine's clientele. Catherine was first, with an article against woman suffrage that stirred up controversy for some time. On 7 May 1870 Calvin Stowe began contributing articles on the New Testament, a series that later broadened its scope and became one of the regular features. In the same issue Harriet also appeared with "Who Ought to Come to Florida?" Meanwhile Mrs. Henry Ward Beecher had already opened her department on "The Household," and she was followed, from time to time, by Thomas K. and all other Beechers who cared to write for publication.

In this congenial family gathering, Harriet apparently felt as thoroughly at home as Henry Ward himself. For his magazine she wrote three serial novels, *My Wife and I, We and Our Neighbors,* and *Poganuc People;* three series of shorter articles that became *Woman in Sacred History, Footsteps of the Master,* and *Palmetto-Leaves;* a share of *Sam Lawson's Oldtown Fireside Stories,* as well as a large number of miscellaneous articles, over fifty of which were never reprinted. From 1870 to her retirement, the *Christian Union* received most of her attention, her happy association with it reflecting or perhaps accounting for the mellowness of her later works.

A few of her miscellaneous unreprinted articles lie outside the realm of her usual topics. Two in this category are "The Indians of St. Augustine," 18 and 25 April 1877, a lively reportorial account of the education of Indians lately brought to Florida from the West. On subjects not entirely new, yet not entirely old, one of the most successful was an obituary notice on Horace Greeley, her old associate from the *Independent,* mixed praise and reservation much more personal than the stereotyped account in *Men of Our Times.* Other obituary notices give evidence of the passing of the years.

Of her old subjects, spiritualism continued to disturb her. Four articles in September and October dealt with this subject, reaching the conclusion that Christianity is more essential to salvation than spiritualism, but that when departed spirits advocate Christian doctrine they may possibly be genuine. This idea was repeated a month later; but a review of Robert Dale Owen's *The Debatable Land,* 29 January 1870, took a negative viewpoint, rejecting spiritualism firmly in favor of Bible revelation.[6]

The familiar lay sermons continue, but it is unnecessary to extend the catalog. She kept her activity and her old interests to the end. She still wrote her travel sketches, from north to south, and she still waxed enthusiastic over chromolithographs such as those given by the *Christian Union* as premiums with subscriptions; she was convinced they could "hardly be distinguished from the originals." She showed herself to be a kindly, alert old lady, greatly concerned with parents who failed to teach their children not to put "Pins in Pussy's Toes," and encouraged by the superior morality shown by the Earl of Beaconsfield in *Lothair*—which she thought, in its improvement over *Vivian Grey,* to be a clear indication of the improved moral standards of British society generally.

She continued to write a little about the former slaves, and a little about prohibition, but without rancor, as now she was inclined to take a hopeful view of the world. As she said, in the last letter (7 February 1877) to the *Christian Union* from Florida: "We are as quiet as a mill-pond. . . . Come down, ye weary, heavy-laden . . . where everybody is good-natured!"

Such was the ending of her literary career. The sweet and gentle *Our Folks at Poganuc,* as it was called in the magazine, ran from 28 November 1877 to 12 June 1878; and her name was not included among the prospective contributors for 1879.

Other Magazines

Of all the magazines for which Stowe wrote regularly, the *Atlantic Monthly* got from her the best work, very likely because it demanded the best. However that may be, when Houghton Mifflin and Company published her *Writings*, they salvaged every scrap from the *Atlantic*, from the innocuous "Mourning-Veil" of the first issue to the explosive "True Story of Lady Byron" and the subsequent *Fireside Stories*. Unfortunately the anonymous editors of the *Writings* were not industrious in searching the files of magazines except their own, so that any important impressions to be gained elsewhere can still be gathered only from the original files.

But there can be no question that her *Atlantic* work is a fair sample of her best efforts. The magazine was so much less provincial than the *Evangelist*, the *Watchman and Reflector*, *Hearth and Home*, or the *Christian Union*, that what she wrote for it is best adapted, on the whole, to give a favorable impression—though not a complete or even an adequate impression—of her work. It took itself seriously as a mouthpiece for American culture and consequently demanded good style as well as good sense. The editors worked over manuscripts conscientiously, preparing them for an eternity within covers as well as for a month on the parlor table. In the *Atlantic* Stowe had the assistance of Lowell, Howells, and others in preparing her stories for posterity.

Of the other magazines that bought her output, Edward Everett Hale's *Old and New* likewise had serious aims but a short life, 1870–1875. Hale, a Unitarian, was the husband of Harriet's niece, the daughter of her sister Mary. Hoping to build circulation, he paid Aunt Harriet well, but he received little from her beyond *Pink and White Tyranny*.[7] Albion Tourgée's *Our Continent*, which was both interesting and short-lived, was a popular literary magazine with special emphasis on the South. To it Stowe made a single contribution, "The Captain's Story," in which she tried her hand at southern local color. *The Revolution* was also a lively little publication—not as inflammatory as it might seem from the title—a magazine for woman's rights conducted by Elizabeth Cady Stanton and Susan B. Anthony. Although it announced Stowe among its contributors, and ran minor contributions from her, it also ran protests against her conservatism.[8] Other contacts, such as that with the important *North American Review*, for which she wrote a single article, are likewise too slight to be of ascertainable significance.[9]

All in all, however, the story of her association with magazines, covering a full half century from 1833 to 1882, is a revealing story of her literary life. Magazines were not only her daily sustenance, but they were the only literary school she ever attended. They may have led her from the path of true artistry, but they made her the figure she became. Without their constant repetition of her name, in their tables of contents and their editorial discussions, she could not have been *the Mrs. Stowe* that everybody came to know and most people came to admire. Never their hack, in the sense of a conscienceless purveyor of whatever was wanted, she was nonetheless their creature.

Chapter Eight

Artistry

A discussion of Harriet Beecher Stowe solely as a literary artist would be brief. The steps by which she became a skillful writer are clear: the example within her family of her father, whose publication of his sermons had begun before her birth; an inspiring teacher; childhood ambitions to versify;[1] letter writing as a family recreation; success among friends as an amateur; her husband's encouragement that she continue her literary efforts; household arrangements for a place and time reserved for writing; preliminary agreements with magazine editors; and eventually a definite program of part-time professionalism. "I am determined not to be a mere domestic slave," she wrote to a friend; "if you see my name coming out everywhere, you may be sure of one thing—that I do it for the pay."[2]

This preparation, undoubtedly effective, included no courses in literary style or literary criticsm, for if the only likely source, John P. Brace, the teacher she eulogized, had emphasized the art of words, young Harriet had not found the subject appealing. Consequently in her mature writings the interest lies in her convictions, her emotions, her hidden depths, but rarely in verbal beauty or mastery of language. Her serious purpose, in fiction as well as in her essays, led her to much soul-searching about what to say, but to few questions about how to say it beautifully.

She had spoken standard English all her life, had studied Murray's grammar book in school, and had taught elementary composition to children before she was twenty, yet in her writings she gave less attention to literary than to culinary art. Why such indifference? We have only hints—not so much an answer as a review of possibilities. In her youth, *fiction* had been a repugnant word, with insinuations of frivolity and indecency. The impression of impropriety grew dim but never vanished, and she still felt uneasy about writing fiction while she was working on her last story. "Even the religious papers are gone mad on serial stories," she complained to her son Charles (CES, 414). "The propensity of the human mind to fiction," she wrote in the preface to an omnibus collec-

tion, *A Library of Famous Fiction,* "is one of those irrepressible forces
against which it has always proved vain to contend."[3] The thought
saddened her, and she recollected that in her youth a favorite subject of
written compositions in the schools had been "On the Disadvantages of
Novel-reading." "Since the world must read fiction," she continued, "let
us have the best in an attractive household form"; that is, in a bowdler-
ized version where, vain as fiction might be, it could avoid vulgarity.
"Swift's genius commands our admiration," she confessed, "but his
words should never be introduced into the home-circle save in such
revised and cleanly editions as the present one" (*LFF,* x).

As editor as well as writer, she found a duty in restraining the
shallow people from worse than folly. *A Library of Famous Fiction,* a
conglomeration dictated by publishing expediency, contained, with its
merely trivial, commercially desirable tales, that gem of gems and
perhaps the only story of which she unreservedly approved, *Pilgrim's
Progress,* which was almost the story of her own life.[4] But by most
readers of fiction, she knew, Bunyan's or her own high standards of
morality was unattainable. The worldliness of the reading public was
one of the "Disadvantages of Novel-writing."

Lady Byron Vindicated (1870)

Though Harriet Beecher Stowe was not endowed with an avid appetite
for literary subtleties, she enjoyed reading. With the same temperament
that permitted her to write rapidly she apparently also read hastily. Most
of her literary references are indefinite, as when, for example, she mentions John Motley as "a man to be proud of" (CES, 415) without a hint of
whether the compliment is due his diplomatic skill, his *History of the
Netherlands,* or his New England birth. After the *Arabian Nights* and the
Waverley novels, only one writer of mere literature moved her deeply,
and she pursued his memory with savage vindictiveness.

Lord Byron, whose glamour fascinated moralists and young girls in
the early nineteenth century, has the honor of being the only author to
whom Stowe devoted a book; and the title, *Lady Byron Vindicated*
(1870), placed the emphasis on the poet's wife. In the two of them
Stowe found echoes of herself: Byron, a kindred imagination tempted
by the Devil; and Lady Byron, a kindred conscience speaking for the
Lord. The book itself, an accidental outgrowth of an indignant article
for the *Atlantic Monthly,* was the offspring of a fascinated horror at the
poet's sinfulness, and of affection for his wife.[5]

Stowe's writings about Byron illustrate many conflicts. In her own mind, she was protecting the memory of a noble wife against the sneers and insults of lewd females and dishonorable males; but to outsiders not conversant with such high morality, she was gratuitously attacking Byron, Thomas Moore, and the manhood of Great Britain. Her excitability (coupled with resultant errors of interpretation) made her recital of essential truth sound like lurid falsehood. Both the original *Atlantic* article and her later expansion exhibited nearly to perfection—in spite of assistance from hired legal and historical consultants—the knack of being unconvincing.

How unjust her opponents were, her own conscience duly advised her. In Lady Byron's words, "Mrs. Stowe, he was guilty of incest with his own sister!" Vainly might she quote this assertion and vainly repeat the answer that she had intended as reassuring. "My dear friend, I have heard that." Long before reaching this point in her narrative, she had lost her case through frantic argumentation and vituperation. The sordid details, instead of substantiating her claims, more deeply prejudiced readers against her. In the controversy that followed, the reliability of her facts was less debated than the incredibility of her own character.[6] When Bayard Taylor asked his friend E. C. Stedman what he thought of *Lady Byron Vindicated,* Stedman replied that Lady Byron was "a jealous virtuous prude" and Stowe "a gossiping green old granny."[7]

In a woman nearing sixty, the adolescent excitement of *Lady Byron Vindicated* is amazing: it was the exasperated outgrowth of a lifelong crush. When she had first read one of his poems—it was "The Corsair," and she was thirteen at the time—she was, as she has said, astonished and electrified; and when she heard that Byron was dead, she prayed and wept as though the world were coming to an end. She was thrilled when, the next Sunday, her father preached a funeral sermon for the dead bard, lamenting his wasted powers. Nor did the memory of Byron fade; for she recalled that her father often said, in his evangelical fervor, that he wished he might have talked to Byron, to straighten the fellow out and make him a harpist for Christ (AF, 38–39).

Harriet herself, at this early age, started a play in blank verse, *Cleon* by name, in which the hero is a dissolute but basically noble youth of the Emperor Nero's court—"the prime companion of our revels," as Nero says. Converted to Christianity, the hero appears to be headed toward martyrdom. Since the play was not completed, the fate of the Byronic hero, whether Christian martyrdom or Christian marriage, remains undisclosed.[8]

During her formative years in Cincinnati, Byron was almost as prominent in the local newspapers as the cholera epidemics. Not only did
frequent short notices appear about his works, but the *Chronicle* on one
occasion (3 November 1832) devoted the entire front page to reprinting
a critical article from a London review. Throughout the first half of her
life, Stowe was continually reminded of what a great, bad man Byron
had been. Her colleague Whittier, writing in the *National Era* (15 July
1847), stated that "in Byron we see Power, uncontrolled by Principle,
Genius divorced from Goodness." This was not only the same moral
estimate of the poet as James Hall's in the *Western Monthly Magazine,*
but the same as her father's in his obituary sermon. Forty-five years
after Byron's death Stowe was also, in a far from delicate way, straight-
ening the fellow out.

In preparation for her *Atlantic* article, Oliver Wendell Holmes, somewhat against his judgment, gave Stowe his "literary counsel and supervi-
sion." To his friend John Motley he wrote, on 18 July 1869, that the
most interesting news he could impart concerned the forthcoming
September *Atlantic.* He predicted, soundly enough, that it would star-
tle the world. "I was not consulted about the matter of publishing Lady
Byron's revelations. Mrs. Stowe assured me that she had made up her
mind about *that.*"[9] Argument, he had learned from experience, was
wasted upon such determination. One questions whether she profited
from the limited criticism she allowed him; for the writing, although
not so slipshod in the article as in the expanded version of the book, was
hysterical and unconvincing.

Few readers, then or since, have agreed with Henry Adams, who
considered it the best work she had done up to that time, ranking it for
effectiveness even above the Topsy scenes of *Uncle Tom's Cabin.* His
statement, however, dates from October 1869, when the excitement
was reaching its height; and, as the full passage in his letter demon-
strates, he was not overcome with admiration for any of her work.[10]
The furor of the moment forgotten, Stowe's entire contribution to the
Byron legend is revelatory primarily of an abiding juvenile fascination
for an abominable gay young devil.

Favorite Writers from the Past

Less spectacular in its effects than Byronism, but pervasive in the
long run, was the influence on Stowe of another romanticist and liberal,
Mme de Staël, whose romance *Corinne; or, Italy* Stowe discovered inde-

pendently in 1833. That this novel, an international best-seller, should have found its way to Cincinnati and into the Beecher household was less remarkable than that it should have awakened such impassioned thought in Harriet Beecher as her letters from the period show. *Corinne; or, Italy* may appear to modern readers either a high-flown demonstration that true love is not smooth or a diluted guidebook to southern Europe, both of which, considered unhistorically, it is; but to Harriet Beecher, in her early twenties, it was a storehouse of wisdom and an ideal of personal perfection. Byron paid *Corinne* the compliment of describing it as more dangerous to virtue than any of his writings, more insidious because it disguised vice under a pious aspiration. It was the veneer that attracted young Harriet.

At the crucial moment of first reading in 1833, Harriet found immediate comfort in the aphorisms liberally sprinkled throughout the book—"The Impassioned are far more liable to weakness than the fickle"—and hope in the question, "Ought not every woman, like every man, to follow the bent of her own talents?" For years the image of Corinne kept reappearing before her: the inspired prophetess raised by purely feminine traits above the blurred half-virtue of a male world. An Americanized Corinne, maternal and matured, remained an ideal for womanhood. The effect was lasting, for as late as 1869 she referred definitely to de Staël's comment on the psychology of English nobility. [11]

Less complicated than her attraction to either Byron or de Staël was Stowe's admiration for Sir Walter Scott, her favorite poet, whose *Lay of the Last Minstrel* she could—and did—recite complete from memory. Nor was her devotion to Scott limited to his poetry. When she was a girl, her father had excepted Scott's prose stories from his general condemnation of novels as trash, and in one summer the family had read *Ivanhoe* seven times. This childhood pleasure in the Waverley novels she renewed with her own children, at one time (1850) reading them all in historical sequence to enliven the routine of history lessons. [12]

The first poetry she had ever read was Scott's ballads, which impressed her much more than Burns's poems, to which she was soon introduced. She liked to contrast Scott with Byron in order to praise the former for his higher morality. "He never makes young ladies feel that they would like to marry corsairs, pirates, or sentimental villains of any description," she wrote in *Sunny Memories* (vol. 1, 143). This judgment she repeated in a later essay for children, "Sir Walter Scott and His Dogs," in which he is mentioned as "one of the greatest geniuses of the world," and Byron as "the great rival poet to Scott . . . not so good or so wise a man by many degrees, but very celebrated in his day."[13] She loved Scott wholeheartedly and was immeasurably fonder of his work than of Shakespeare's.

Stowe's visit to Stratford was the duty call demanded by a great reputation. Although professing conventional admiration, she squirmed under the coarseness in Shakespeare's plays; she doubted the accuracy of his history; and she looked disapprovingly on his frivolity. On the whole, she was repelled most by the "weirdness" of his writing. She feared that he lacked a progressive mind for enthusiastic reform, and she softened to him only when thinking of Queen Elizabeth, "this most repulsive and disagreeable woman," the "belligerent old Gorgon" whose gross taste had disgraced her entire court and period.[14] *The Tempest* was an exception, for she quoted approvingly from it in *The Minister's Wooing,* in *The Pearl of Orr's Island,* and in "A Student's Sea Story," from *Sam Lawson's Oldtown Fireside Stories.* The attractions of *The Tempest* were the innocence of Miranda and the beauty of the lyric "Full fathom five."

Like Shakespeare, Milton—an old favorite of her father—failed to impress her deeply, although she did respect "Il Penseroso." In *Sunny Memories* she called him "cold" (vol. 1, 207; vol. 2, 2, 279), and apparently preferred Dr. Watts, "a born poet" (vol 2., 27). Although Milton is referred to in *Uncle Tom's Cabin* and in *The Minister's Wooing,* he is prominently mentioned only in *Oldtown Folks* (268, 422, 433, 435, 442, 447, 477, 501, 604). In it he becomes a definite symbol of Puritanism, comparable in significance to the New England divines, Bellamy, Edwards, Eliot, and Hopkins.

She knew large parts of the Bible well, of course, and could paraphrase it, make an allusion or reference, or quote a verse whenever she wished. It was not secular literature but God's word, to be studied devoutly for salvation. She also knew and certainly enjoyed hymns and sacred songs, for she quoted from enough of them, year after year, to fill an anthology.[15]

A list of all Stowe's casual literary references would be long, for her reading was not deficient in quantity, however superficial her responses seem to have been.[16] She obviously admired Samuel Richardson more than casually (though she never suggested that his psychological subtlety appealed to her) and had been willing to skip a dinner invitation to plunge once more into the enchanting pages of *Sir Charles Grandison.* She mentions this book in *The Minister's Wooing* as inevitable in the library of the well-taught young woman of the late eighteenth century, along with the *Spectator, Robinson Crusoe,* the Bible, and the writings of Jonathan Edwards.[17] Edgeworth was another permanent favorite, both for her novels and for her stories for children. It was only at maturity that she dipped into Chaucer. "I read Chaucer a great deal yesterday, and am charmed at the reverential Christian spirit in which he viewed all things."[18]

Contemporaries

If Stowe's taste for the great writers of the past was conventional in its limitations, her taste for her contemporaries was no less so. She was surprised during her first visit in England at the respect she found for Emerson, Hawthorne, and Prescott, none of whom she had discovered herself. Hawthorne she at first viewed with skepticism, and it was only after overcoming her distrust of his strange viewpoint that she could unqualifiedly endorse him after his death as a "wonderful fellow" and "our most exquisite writer."[19] She never reconciled herself to Emerson, her father's early feuds with the Unitarians predisposing her against anything that smacked of transcendentalism.

For Holmes and Whittier, on the other hand, she had from the first personal and hence literary liking. The two men had both been associated with the *Atlantic* from its earliest days, and Whittier had also been a contributing editor to the *National Era* and to the *Independent.* With the good doctor she carried on an extended and vivacious exchange of letters, over thirty pages of which, on Holmes's side, can be found in the memoir of his life.

Stowe was also greatly attached to Elizabeth Barrett Browning, whom she met in Italy; what she thought of Robert, or he of her, remains a matter of surmise. Her friendship with George Eliot, important to both of them, was based on mutual admiration nurtured by tolerance on both sides. "A Dog's Mission," one of Harriet's moral tales for children, is by imitation a tribute to *Silas Marner.* In this parable a hard-hearted old maid, Zarviah Avery by name, is restored to natural sympathy by the intrusion into her life of a stray dog. Gradually her circle of tolerance extends from dogs to children; and at the end of the tale she is reconciled to her brother (whom she had driven out of her house to California in his childhood) and, like Silas Marner, to the entire human race.[20]

Among the prominent literary men of her time, Lowell was the most important to her. As editor of the *Atlantic,* he was able to adopt the tone of personal interest that she esteemed so highly. His love of the old New England was as strong as hers, and, best of all, he praised her work extravagantly. *The Minister's Wooing* was, according to his words (or at least according to the impression he tried to give through them), an imperishable masterpiece.[21] Whittier was much sounder in saying of the story to Lowell that it opened with promise but that it was thin, lacking the fullness of detail necessary to let the reader know in what part of the world he was supposed to find himself, in what age, and in what climate.[22]

If contemporary writers were not a chief influence on Stowe's work, there was also a perceptible shade of condescension in their attitude toward her. She was in the New England group without really being accepted by it, a rejection partly the result of her sex and partly of her principles. How she was denied their full confidence is indicated in the letter Charles Eliot Norton wrote Arthur Hugh Clough about the forthcoming new magazine, the *Atlantic*. After naming Motley, Holmes, Emerson, and Lowell as contributors, Norton mentioned the projected policy of printing most articles anonymously, using authors' names only when the names were worth more than the articles. The first issue, he said, would contain two such articles: one of them was to be Stowe's.[23]

A more spectacular example of the distinction the eminent gentlemen drew between themselves and Stowe is afforded by the records of an *Atlantic* dinner of 1859, to which, after considerable trepidation, the women contributors had been invited. Only two ladies appeared, Harriet Prescott and Stowe, who had accepted on condition that no wine was to be served. As Lowell wrote to Emerson, this proviso tied a witches'-knot; and the manner in which the gentlemen hoodwinked the prohibitionist by serving themselves wine in water glasses has been told with richly genteel humor by Thomas Wentworth Higginson, one of the unregenerate participants in the ruse.

After a cold, wineless start, the party livened a bit, as Lowell assured Stowe that *Tom Jones* was the best novel ever written and Holmes tried to convince Professor Stowe that profanity had originated in the free use of language in the pulpit. Both of the Stowes were heard to observe later that they had been disappointed in the dinner; for, while the company was undoubtedly distinguished, "the conversation was not quite what they had been led to expect."[24]

A sermon could be based on this incident, for Harriet in private life was not the abstainer she seemed. She advocated temperance in her stories and described the wretched victims of alcohol, but at home she benefited from a little wine, provided the quality was good, taken early in the morning as medicine and tonic. The moral distinction between group drinking for sociability and private drinking for energy needs a Beecher theologian's attention.

Professional envy was a vicious trait completely alien to Stowe's character. She was invariably kindly and generous toward young writers (except French novelists whom she never named) and humanitarian reformers. Books for which she wrote introductory notes reveal her tastes: *An Inside View of Slavery* by C. G. Parsons (1855); the *Works of Charlotte Elizabeth Tonna* (1844–45);[25] *Tell it All: The Story of a Life's Experiences in Mormonism* by T. B. H. Stenhouse (1874); *The Incarnation; or, Pictures of the Virgin and her Son,* by Charles Beecher (1849). She occasionally reviewed or discussed in her magazine departments books on spiritualism and theology, and she thought well enough of A. D. T. Whitney, the author of *Faith Gartney's Girlhood* (1863) and other books for girls, to write a biographical sketch for an omnibus volume called *Our Famous Women* (1884), in which she also published a sketch of her sister Catherine.

In her later years, although she liked *The Luck of Roaring Camp* volume by Bret Harte and praised the local-color sketches of George Washington Cable,[26] she was more gushingly enthusiastic about fiction with a stronger evangelical appeal. Among lesser-known novels, she was carried away by a certain *What Answer?* (1868) by Anna Dickinson, a woman of varied talents, mostly of a performing sort, among which writing fiction was not included. This novel, dealing with the social effects of miscegenation, was greeted by Stowe as "a noble deed," to the great disgust of the New York *Nation,* which responded that *What Answer?* was "emphatically a bad novel—without interest, even possessing some positive qualities which inflict pain on any one who in the least values art." This was a criticism that Stowe had already discounted. "Works of art be hanged! You had a braver thought than that." Despite such endorsements by Stowe and Lydia Maria Child, the "noble deed" failed. What remained was Stowe's encouragement. "Your poor old grandma in this work rejoices to find it in your brave young hands."[27]

Still another reforming novel that she praised with possibly excessive enthusiasm was *Environment: A Story of Modern Society,* by her biographer, Florine Thayer McCray. "It is truly a *Christian* story," she wrote, 27 July 1887. "The alcohol which wrought all the mischief and danger was prescribed and *insisted on* by a doctor!" The italics are Stowe's. "I *must* express the hope that your book will be widely and *thoughtfully* read and do the good it was evidently intended to do."[28]

Limitations of Craftsmanship

That *Uncle Tom's Cabin,* Stowe's first novel, should have the strongest construction, as well as the richest content, of any of her novels, shows an uncommon inability to profit from the experience of writing. Nothing exhibits more clearly her limited conception of the art than the seven articles on reading and writing for *Hearth and Home* (1869). "Can I Write?," the first of these, bravely gives practical advice to beginners. Initial attempts should be on a small scale, she advised, recalling her own introduction to the writing business. Writing, to be profitable, must be directed toward a particular magazine or editor. A suitable subject for a young woman would be, "How to quiet a fretful baby."

A week later she proceeded to the question, "How Shall I Learn to Write?" First, by having something to say, she decided; second, by practicing expression. Much can be learned from the careful study of Hawthorne's *American Notebooks.* This excellent if unexpected advice was followed by a pertinent view of "Faults of Inexperienced Writers." Here she commented soundly on the vices of indefiniteness, unreasonably big words, and unconscious imitation.

These two articles, a promising introduction, proved to contain her total rhetorical teaching, for the following week in "How May I Know That I May Make a Writer?" she could invoke only the commercial test. If you have a genius for writing, she said, people will be glad to pay you. "Writing—Commercially," a month and a half later, restated this view. Writing is worth, she repeated, whatever it will bring. Shrewd as these comments are from the commercial angle that was her natural perspective, the food they offer literary art is skimpy. To say what one thinks editors want, and in language readers understand, summarizes her advice.

As her truest admirers have pointed out, Stowe was not adept at writing. "A woman like Mrs. Stowe," Jewett wrote charitably, "cannot bring herself to that cold selfishness of the moment for one's work's sake."[29] The pioneer unauthorized biographer, McCray, aware of the imperfections of her idol's writings, was sorrowfully convinced that, despite their genius, they were not stylistic triumphs. "How marvellous a figure in literary history would Harriet Beecher Stowe have been," she lamented, "could she also have been cited as a model of writing, like Thackeray, Irving, or Lydia Maria Child!" (327). Annie Fields points to the same fact without invoking the same hallowed names.

Stowe's lifetime of writing led to no sure stylistic improvement over her childhood prize-winning composition on natural morality. Throughout her life she had merely, as she once described her method of work, plunged boldly into the discussion of abstruse subjects. Her editor, James T. Fields, who described her habits as "peculiarly her own," commented in astonishment on her powers of concentration. "She *croons,* so to speak, over her writings, and it makes very little difference to her whether there is a crowd of people about her or whether she is alone during the composition of her books."[30] Elizabeth Cady Stanton, the feminist leader, offers another example of Stowe's ability to isolate herself in a world of her own. Calling on her, Stanton found her in her sanctum, writing *Lady Byron Vindicated,* while her sister Catherine, in the same room, was also writing. Without any disturbance, the Beecher women dropped their literary work, while Catherine explained to Stanton her objections to woman suffrage.[31]

Stowe's assertions of trancelike absorption in her work are borne out by the evidence. After it was printed, she revised nothing; before it was printed, she seldom rewrote for exactness. Her comments on *Oldtown Folks*—and her defense when her publisher was impatiently requesting the promised copy—are almost unique in her correspondence, "I am bound by the laws of art," she insisted. "Instead of rushing on, I have often turned back and written over with care, that nothing that I wanted to say might be omitted; it has cost me a good deal of labor to elaborate this first part, namely, to build my theatre and to introduce my actors. My labor has all, however, been given to the literary part."[32]

Such efforts were out of the ordinary. According to her own testimony she never bothered to use the elementary tools of punctuation and grammar correctly.[33] She never tried to master other less elementary tools of expression, being indifferent to her writing except for the amorphous *good* it would do. William Dean Howells, recalling his struggles with her manuscript when he was working on the *Atlantic Monthly,* wrote with gentle frankness of her carelessness. The combined labors of the magazine staff were invoked to polish her manuscripts. The under proofreader; the head reader; Howells, verifying quotations, dates, names; the printer; the head reader again; Howells once more;

and finally the head reader, for a last revision—these were the interme-
diaries between an author and the fastidious readers of the *Atlantic*. For
Stowe's contributions, he revealed, the text was often "largely rewrit-
ten" on the proof-sheets.[34]

Such time-consuming labors of stylistic refinement were obviously
dispensed with in her other writings, which, like *We and Our Neighbors*
or *Pink and White Tyranny*, represent more faithfully her status as
literary craftsman. As she read books approaching them like timetables
to find out where they would take her, so she wrote books, regarding
them as marketable commodities, for what they would get her.[35]

As the result of this attitude toward her works, her comments on
them are singularly unenlightening. "We write only as we are driven,
and never know exactly where we are going to land," reads a sentence of
confession from *The Minister's Wooing* (27). "When the mind is full of
one thing, why go about to write on another?" she asked, in the one
comment on writing in *Palmetto-Leaves* (161). As a fictionist she discovered only one principle about herself: that at certain times she could
succeed better than at others. She regarded herself as the lucky recipient
of fitful inspiration. "When the spirits will help, I can write," was still
her attitude in 1868, after thirty years of literary endeavor (AF, 315).
More important perhaps to explain the stodgy inequalities of her stories
is her conception of them as not primarily stories: they were guidebooks
to New England or unwilling dilutions of moralizing into "serials," the
shapeless monsters that made much of her life a nightmare.

In this point of view, it must be granted, there was common sense;
for she found it difficult to combine things she wanted to say with an
artificially imposed plot that, as likely as not, pointed in some vastly
different direction. And so it was wise of her to consider her books from
a utilitarian viewpoint. In a letter to a friend about *Men of Our Times*,
she exclaimed that the book, "hang it!" was almost done (AF, 306). She
was fully satisfied with it, having discovered that she could write
biographies to order, the lives of model beings that would inspire
young men and women. If only her books could have accomplished
what she wanted, she would have been fully justified in her self-
satisfaction. To her, at least, they were not hack writing but Service.

Chapter Nine
Afterword

Harriet Beecher Stowe's last years need no long recounting in a survey of her literary career. Hers was not the ideal old age she had described in "The Mourning-Veil," her contribution to the first issue of the *Atlantic*. "God sometimes gives to good men a guileless and holy second childhood, in which the soul becomes childlike, not childish, and the faculties in full fruit and ripeness are mellow without sign of decay." Though she was surrounded by love and material comfort until her death in 1896, her intellect collapsed years before. At the end, she was merely pathetic. Mark Twain has described her as wandering about Hartford—for after 1884, infirmity, first her husband's then her own, had prevented the annual winter visits to Florida. Sometimes he saw her under the care of an attendant and sometimes sneaking about alone, entering the neighbors' houses, drumming to herself on their pianos or startling them with sudden war whoops.[1]

Before her complete mental collapse, Stowe was enabled, for the first time, to live a restful, unhurried life. Even in Hartford, the scene of her girlhood suffering in sister Catherine's school, she carried with her the inner peace of her calm isle of Patmos. With no more serial stories to be written for younger generations and no new moral revelations to guide them, she was content to leave to them the work of the world, pridefully quoting from her childhood favorite, "My sword I give to him that shall succeed me in my pilgrimage and my courage and skill to him that can get it." Whatever her reservations may have been, the old reformer, belated discoverer of a nature that was not Calvinistic, escaped the harsh melancholy that, she recalled, Cotton Mather had attributed to aged New Englanders. No longer scolding the human race or improving it with pulpit evangelism, she would calmly view it, freed from concern for either its momentary problems or its ultimate destiny.

She was not a new woman, surprising as her transformation appears, for this autumn mood was not entirely the creation of her last years. The privilege of indulging it continually, which was new, was in itself enough to alter her character amazingly. She became pure "home body," the private woman that nature had intended and life so cruelly prevented. Lucy Larcom, who met the older woman in 1862—when Stowe was barely past fifty—had encountered her in a peaceful moment that presaged the mood of the last years. "It was as beautiful as a page from one of her story books," Larcom noted, referring to the lunch hour. The old stone house at Andover, the golden August day, the thoughtful table arrangements, seen through the hero-worshipping eyes of the yet unrecognized poetess, reached a quiet perfection that remained one of the pleasantest recollections of her life.[2]

A less sentimental observer, William Dean Howells, has also testified to Stowe's charm. "Mrs. Stowe was a gracious person," he wrote in reminiscences of his Boston days. He did not know her well, but enough to realize that she was simple, motherly, and "divinely sincere." As he saw her most, before her mental collapse, she was the quiet figure with the "inalienable charm" of her later years.[3]

As an old lady she exhaled continually a modest spiritual dignity far more impressive than the nagging insistence of her younger, active years. "What are queer old women for," Miss Mehitable had asked in *Oldtown Folks,* "if young folks may not have a good laugh out of them now and then?" Had she retained her vigor to the end, she might have been the queer old woman of her foreboding soul; but, as her life turned out, one is less tempted to laugh the older she grows. "I think generally we take ourselves altogether too seriously," Miss Mehitable had offered in explanation of her question. Stowe's lines from her poem "The Secret" could have appropriately been Stowe's last wish.

> O rest of rests! O peace serene, eternal!
> Thou ever livest and thou changest never;
> And in the secret of the presence dwelleth
> Fullness of joy, forever and forever.[4]

Unlike his wife, old professor Stowe, as his years advanced, developed a more crotchety disposition and a more grotesque exterior. To Susy Clemens he was Santa Claus: with his portly frame, his lumbering walk, his glorious white bushy whiskers, and his pink little nose—later it withered into a misformed mass—his physical likeness to the children's Christmas friend needed only a red cotton suit to be made perfect. Calvin Stowe was not the careless, absentminded soul he appeared to observers, for Jonathan Edwards still governed his melancholy thoughts.

His celebrated wife, though she had never been acclaimed a beauty, was a sweet-looking old lady. On her last public appearance she had been the guest at a formal reception arranged by her publishers to honor her seventieth birthday. For this farewell, tributes had been composed by her admirers, among others Whittier and dear Dr. Holmes; and her beloved Henry Ward had come to hear her final comments on the success of Negro emancipation. Her biographers can linger affectionately over the occasion, rich in symbolism of the fading light of her antebellum fame, vivid only in the recollections of other survivors from the same distant era; but commentators have regretted that she had become complacent in accepting the continued injustices of the later period.

In her private life too she bade the world farewell, sorting through her papers, destroying some and passing the selected remainder on to her son Charles Edward. They would be her biography, and she often hoped that the two of them might manage a collaborative work, which she would call *Pebbles from the Shores of a Past Life,* like the book she and the other children had arranged from her father's last conversations and carefully preserved journals and correspondence. "The desire to leave behind me some recollections of my life, has been cherished by me, for many years past; but failing strength and increasing infirmities"—she was writing from Hartford, 30 September 1889—"have prevented its accomplishment."[5]

In her senility, especially after her return to Hartford in 1884, a kind of wisdom of the sage possessed her. In the note she composed as a foreword to her son's biography of her, she was still hoping that the book might do good in leading its readers to "a firmer trust in God and a deeper sense of his fatherly goodness"; yet accompanying this old ambition was the new realization of personal inadequacy. "It is perhaps much more accurate as to detail and impression than is possible with any autobiography written late in life." The task, she might have been saying, was gladly resigned by one who had learned its unimportance.

As a woman, Harriet Beecher Stowe represented the type she most admired and whom she praised so obsessively, those women for whom family and God were masters; she was not so vain that she necessarily considered herself the perfect example of the type. As a legendary abolitionist, either absurd fanatic or heroine of freedom, she took her place in the ranks of American folk characters alongside her Topsy and Eva and Uncle Tom. She will not be dislodged as long as *Uncle Tom's Cabin* remains fruitfully controversial. Whether her other books will be read much more, except by antiquarians, is problematic. New points of interest have been discovered in her writings lately, ensuring more attention by critics and scholars, if not by the public at large. If unsolicited and sincere testimonials could sell a book, *Oldtown Folks* would be near the top of the list of old-fashioned classics. Many distinguished reputations—those of Longfellow, Whittier, Irving, Cooper—rest on a less solid foundation.

In the reinterpretation of the past, a periodic if not constant process, Stowe's position among her contemporaries may continue to shift. Her undoubted though undetermined influence in the abolition movement is not her only significance. She spoke on other subjects and for other people—for women under the heel of masculine domination, for children under the burden of adult repression, and for lowly humanity. Her efforts deserve attention and will reward the observer.

Although Stowe was an intelligent and clever writer, she had no aesthetic standards, for herself or others. Genial old professor Barrett Wendell was both accurate and kindly (also possibly condescending) when he stated that she "differed from most American novelists in possessing a spark of genius" or "gleams of creative genius." If she could have been other than she was, "she might have been a figure of lasting literary importance" with "a distinguished place in English fiction"; instead, her stories are rambling and uneven, with only certain "carefully deliberate passages," like the opening chapters of *Oldtown Folks* (with their inestimable debt to Calvin Stowe), "written in a manner which approaches excellence."[6] The word Wendell should have used is *elegance,* or stylistic neatness.

Negative appraisals of Stowe's writing are unavoidable and so prevalent that they cannot be denied. Too often she wrote as she had learned in the early days before *Uncle Tom's Cabin* and her liberation. Her flat expression can be deadly. She never appreciated the significance of such a concept as "the fortunate fall." There was nothing like Emerson's "Brahma" in her universe. The Faust theme—the symbol of a man who could cooperate with the Devil and yet achieve ethical greatness—was alien to her thought and did not interest her much. Unlike Emerson, Hawthorne, Melville, or Whitman, she never suspected that sin might also somehow contribute to morality.

Although Stowe's writing shows hidden impulses in conflict with her simplified values, it lacks the verbal magic and the complexity of images to keep much of it alive. From youth to age she wrote lively scenes, expressed provocative ideas, created brisk dialogue, none of which anthologize well. She wrote for her time, not ours; for her magazines, not ours. She offers qualified readers quiet entertainment and a wealth of information, but a major modification of literary standards will be required to move her to a position of high critical esteem. Only *Uncle Tom's Cabin* —assuredly a miracle, magnificent or monstrous—written in anguish and frustration, is adequately equipped with symbols, paradoxes, concealed associations, tensions, equivalences, ambiguity, and the paraphernalia of significant expression. More levels of meaning can be observed in a single story like Hawthorne's "Young Goodman Brown" or Poe's "Fall of the House of Usher" than in an entire novel by Stowe. On the documentary level, however, she offers to qualified readers— particularly in *Oldtown Folks*—a wealth of information about our earlier United States and some of the curious kinds of people who were involved in making it what it is.

Notes and References

Chapter One

1. Gunnar Myrdal observes that women and children have been "suppressed" in almost every society because their "high social visibility" makes them easy targets. ("A Parallel to the Negro Problem," appendix 5, in *An American Dilemma: The Negro Problem and Modern Democracy,* 20th-anniversary ed. [New York: Harper & Row, 1962], 1073–78). Blanche Glassman Hersh is more specific throughout her book, *The Slavery of Sex: Feminist-Abolitionists in America* (Urbana: University of Illinois Press, 1978).

2. As described in the Selected Bibliography, the most useful biographies of Harriet Beecher Stowe (HBS) for reference purposes are by Charles Edward Stowe, *Life of Harriet Beecher Stowe Compiled from Her Letters and Journals* (Boston: Houghton, Mifflin, 1889); Annie Fields, *Life and Letters of Harriet Beecher Stowe* (Boston: Houghton, Mifflin, 1898); and Forrest Wilson, *Crusader in Crinoline: The Life of Harriet Beecher Stowe* (Philadelphia: J. B. Lippincott, 1941). These are indicated in my notes and text by the authors' names or initials: CES, AF, FW. Also valuable is the later book by Milton Rugoff, *The Beechers: An American Family in the Nineteenth Century* (New York: Harper and Row, 1981).

3. The strongest indictment of Lyman Beecher's educational practices is made by Barbara M. Cross in the preface to her edition of his *Autobiography* (Cambridge, Mass: Harvard University Press, 1961), xii–xxxiii.

4. Theological questions, of primary importance in most of Stowe's writings, are expertly discussed in Charles H. Foster's *The Rungless Ladder: Harriet Beecher Stowe and New England Puritanism* (Durham, N.C.: Duke University Press, 1954).

5. Lyman Beecher Stowe, *Saints, Sinners, and Beechers* (Indianapolis: Bobbs-Merrill, 1934), 163.

Chapter Two

1. "Love *versus* Law," in *The Mayflower; or, Sketches of Scenes and Characters among the Descendants of the Puritans* (New York: Harper & Brothers, 1843), 54; hereafter cited in the text as *MF.* The original title of the story, as published in *The Gift* for 1840, was "Deacon Enos."

2. Ibid., 87–88. The italics are HBS's.

3. *Dred: A Tale of the Great Dismal Swamp* (Boston: Phillips, Sampson 1856), vol. 2, 42; hereafter cited in the text as *Dred.* Calvin Stowe had also been a college valedictorian.

4. Catherine M. Sedgwick was an important writer, as Mary Kelley says, "perhaps the most important single figure" studied in her book, *Private Woman, Public Stage: Literary Domesticity in Nineteenth-Century America* (New York: Oxford University Press, 1984), a study that includes Warner, Cummins, and Stowe. Sedgwick's novel, *A New England Tale* (1822; rpt., New York: J.C. Derby, 1854), is an example of regionalism similar to that of Sigourney and early Stowe. See Nina Baym, *Woman's Fiction* (Ithaca, N.Y: Cornell University Press, 1978), 54–56. Baym is one of the half-dozen contributors who discuss or comment on Stowe's work in the *Columbia Literary History of the United States* (New York: Columbia University Press, 1988); see particularly 305.

5. Lydia Huntley Sigourney, *Sketch of Connecticut, Forty Years Since* (Hartford: Oliver D. Cooke & Sons, 1824), 4.

6. Ibid, 110.

7. Ibid, 112.

8. Harriet E. Beecher, *A New England Sketch* (Lowell, Mass: Alfred Gilman, 1834); reverse of title page.

9. James Hall, *Illinois Monthly Magazine* 1 (1831), 19.

10. James Hall, *Western Monthly Magazine* 1 (1833), 2–3.

11. Ibid., 8–9.

12. *Western Monthly Magazine* 1 (1833): 287.

13. "Isabelle and Her Sister Kate and Their Cousin," *Western Monthly Magazine* 2 (February 1834), 72–75.

14. The financial failure of the *Western Monthly Magazine* was caused by a religious controversy with Lyman Beecher; see John T. Flanagan, *James Hall, Literary Pioneer of the Ohio Valley* (Minneapolis: University of Minnesota Press, 1941), 66–67. Randolph C. Randall (*James Hall: Spokesman of the New West* [Columbus: Ohio State University Press, 1964], chapter 13, 225–28) recounts the history of the *Western Monthly Magazine*, with information about Stowe's contributions.

15. Edward Deering Mansfield, *Personal Memoirs* (Cincinnati: Robert Clarke & Co., 1879), 295.

16. The four stories were reprinted from *Godey's Lady's Book;* see Lyle H. Wright, *American Fiction 1774–1850* (San Marino, Calif.: Huntington Library, 1939), 124–25.

17. "The Yankee Girl," in HBS, *Regional Sketches: New England and Florida,* ed. John R. Adams (New Haven, Conn.: College and University Press, 1972), 62–74. Edward Wagenknecht provides a synopsis in his book, *Harriet Beecher Stowe: The Known and the Unknown* (New York: Oxford University Press, 1965), 231 n.7; and Josephine Donovan discusses it as "the most significant of Stowe's early stories" (*New England Local Color Literature* [New York: Frederick Ungar Publishing Co., 1983], 55).

18. "The Tea Rose," *Godey's Lady's Book* 28 (1839): 115–22, and re-

printed by Sarah Josepha Hale in *Woman's Record* (New York: Harper & Brothers, 1852), a comprehensive annotated anthology.

19. The Hale anthology shows the state of affairs, as do Rufus Wilmot Griswold's *The Female Poets of America*, 1849 (enl. ed., New York: James Miller, 1877), and John S. Hart's *The Female Prose Writers of America* (Philadelphia: E. H. Butler and Co., 1852), in which "The Tea-Rose" represents Stowe.

20. Read sympathetically, *The Wide, Wide World* can still be interesting for its local color as well as for the conviction of its religious and domestic themes. Edward Halsey Foster offers a complete analysis of the book (*Susan and Ann Warner* [Boston: Twayne, n.d.], 34–53. See also Baym, *Woman's Fiction*, 143–50; and Joanne Dobson, "The Hidden Hand: Subversion of Cultural Ideology in Three Mid-Nineteenth-Century Women's Novels," *American Quarterly* 38 (1986): 223–42.

21. *The Lamplighter* (1854) by Maria S. Cummins is the novel often cited as an example of sentimental resignation, but Prentiss goes far beyond Cummins in resignation to mistreatment. Moreover, Prentiss's dialogue is less stilted, her scenes are sharper, and her moral is more obvious.

22. The passage quoted here of *Stepping Heavenward* is from the end of the story of a Whitman Publishing Co. edition (Racine, Wisc., n.d.). Both *The Wide, Wide World* and *Stepping Heavenward* were available in cheap reprints a few years ago. Although *Stepping Heavenward* has been ignored by historians of the art of fiction (for good reason), it is noted with a measure of justice by Willard Thorpe in his survey "The Religious Novel as Best Seller in America," in *Religion in American Life*, ed. J. W. Smith and A. L. Jamison (Princeton, N.J.: Princeton University Press, 1961), vol. 2, 211–12. See also Ann Douglas, *The Feminization of American Culture* (New York: Knopf, 1977), 215–17.

Chapter Three

1. *Uncle Tom's Cabin; or, Life among the Lowly* (Boston: Houghton, Osgood, 1878). This edition has the advantages over the first edition of easier accessibility and an extensive author's introduction. All my page references are to this edition; my chapter references are to any edition. A fine recent edition is published by the Harvard University Press (Cambridge, Mass., 1962), with an authoritative introduction by Kenneth S. Lynn. The paperback Penguin American Library edition (New York, 1981) reprints the Harvard text with a new introduction by Ann Douglas. A combination of synopsis and analysis is common among writers on *Uncle Tom's Cabin* (*UTC*); a satisfactory brief example is by Moira Davison Reynolds in chapter 2, "A Noble Work," of her book *"Uncle Tom's Cabin" and Mid-Nineteenth Century United States: Pen and Conscience* (Jefferson, N.C.: McFarland & Co., Inc., 1985), 13–42. The best and most complete example is by Thomas F. Gossett in his *"Uncle Tom's Cabin" and American Culture* (Dallas: Southern Methodist University Press, 1985), a big book that every reader with serious interest in *UTC* should consult.

2. Critics are reluctant to believe that the title was chosen because it is a catchy phrase, or that it was selected before the author knew the direction her serial would take. Egbert S. Oliver, in "The Little Cabin of Uncle Tom" (*College English* 26 [1964–65]: 355–61), finds that "cabin" is a symbol of "the family center" and that its position in the title announces the importance of family life in the story. Donald K. Pickens also uses the cabin as symbol in a sarcastic sentence. "In this pre-Freudian classic the cabin had a kitchen but not a bedroom" (*Negro American Literary Forum* 3 [1969]: 47). Among other symbolic interpretations, Philip Fisher discovers irony in "uncle" as well as in "cabin" (*Hard Facts* [New York: Oxford University Press, 1985], 119–20). The second subtitle (Life among the Lowly) has been accepted without question as an improvement over the first (The Man That Was a Thing).

3. *First Geography for Children* (Boston: Phillips, Sampson, 1855), 42: "God always makes those most prosperous who are most obedient to his laws in the Bible. The New England people own more ships, in proportion to their numbers, than any other country; and manufactories like those in the picture [on page 40 of the geography] abound all over New England, especially in Massachusetts." The conception of a vicious class struggle in the capitalistic North probably stemmed from the South's leading statesman, John C. Calhoun, "the Marx of the master class," who had been expressing the idea for years before his death in 1850. See Richard N. Current, *John C. Calhoun* (New York: Twayne, 1963), 88, 90, 101, 162.

4. See Karen Halttunen, "Gothic Imagination and Social Reform: The Haunted House of Lyman Beecher, Henry Ward Beecher, and Harriet Beecher Stowe," in *New Essays on "Uncle Tom's Cabin,"* ed. Eric J. Sundquist (New York: Cambridge University Press, 1986). Halttunen ascribes the horror of Legree's plantation to Harriet's childhood fascination with her father's sermons.

5. The phenomenal sales of *UTC* are estimated by James D. Hart, *The Popular Book: A History of America's Literary Taste* (New York: Oxford University Press, 1950), 110–12; and by Frank Luther Mott, *Golden Multitudes: The Story of Best Sellers in the United States* (New York: Macmillan, 1957), 117–21. See also Susan Geary, "The Domestic Novel as a Commercial Commodity: Making a Best Seller in the 1850s," *Papers of the Bibliographical Society of America* 70 (1976): 365–93, 375–77.

6. Disputes about originals have fascinated literal-minded antiquarians. Sources for Eliza have been claimed by the family biographies and by HBS in the "Concluding Remarks" of *UTC;* yet the Eliza of the book is, as HBS clearly understood, the projection of the author's feelings as a mother. Though Topsy may have been suggested by a servant whom HBS knew at some time, in the book Topsy became less a human being than a minstrel show stereotype or, perhaps as Leslie Fiedler suggested, a symbolic picturesque blackness to balance the pure whiteness of Eva (*No! in Thunder* [Boston: Beacon Press, 1960], 267).

7. Lyman Beecher, *Autobiography* (New York: Harper & Brothers, 1864), vol. 2, 345.

8. Theodore Dwight Weld, *American Slavery as It Is; Testimony of a Thousand Witnesses* (New York: American Anti-Slavery Society, 1839). The letter, quoted by Gilbert Hobbs Barnes, *The Antislavery Impulse, 1830–1844* (New York: D. Appleton-Century Co., 1933), 231, is genuine, but HBS may have been mistaken about how much she used Weld's book for *UTC*. See Gossett, *"Uncle Tom's Cabin" and American Culture*, 437 n. 3.

9. An article by Evan Branstadter, "Uncle Tom and Archy Moore: The Anti-Slavery Novel as Ideological Symbol" (*American Quarterly* 26 [1974]: 160–75), is a thorough treatment of the subject, with an analysis of Hildreth's novel, identifications of similarities to and differences from Stowe's, including Hildreth's later comments on *Uncle Tom's Cabin*. Charles Nicols, writing in *Phylon* 19 (1958): 325–34, ventures further than most readers. "It seems to me that Harriet Beecher Stowe's chief source was Hildreth's *The Slave*" (330).

10. Several research articles on early antislavery fiction give information on possible influences on *UTC:* Nicholas Canady, Jr., "The Anti-slavery Novel prior to 1852 and Hildreth's *The Slave* (1856)," *College Language Association Journal* 17 (1973–74): 175–96; Jules Zanger, "The 'Tragic Octoroon' in Pre–Civil War Fiction," *American Quarterly* 18 (1966): 63–70; Tremaine McDowell, "The Negro in the Southern Novel Prior to 1850" (1926), reprinted in *Images of the Negro in American Literature*, ed. Seymour L. Gross and John Edward Hardy [Chicago: University of Chicago Press, 1966], 54–70.

11. Baym describes Southworth's *Retribution* in *Woman's Fiction*, 118–20.

12. The vital importance of the Fugitive Slave Act is unquestioned. See Gossett, *"Uncles Tom's Cabin" and American Culture*, 87 and elsewhere. As late as 1905 a sturdy southerner charged that the book was subsidized. "The faithful guardians of American union had *Uncle Tom's Cabin* written on purpose to prevent the execution of the fugitive slave law" (John C. Reed, of Georgia, *The Brothers' War* [Boston: Little, Brown and Co., 1905], 183).

13. Henry James, *A Small Boy and Others* (London: Macmillan, 1913), 263.

14. Not everybody liked *UTC*, or ever will. The charges of "Uncle Tomism," revived by James Baldwin's brilliant 1949 essay in *Partisan Review* (16 [June 1949]: 578–85] and developed by Joseph C. Furnas in his book *Goodbye to Uncle Tom* (New York: W. Sloane Associates, 1956) have a basis in fact, though as Furnas admits, Stowe's "puerilities" were "inadvertent" and she was not responsible for the "destructive racism" of George Aiken's stage adaptation. At the time she wrote, Stowe's tacit assumption of white superiority did not indicate hostility. She had been taught from childhood that New Englanders were the chosen people, superior to all other whites; yet she felt that Negroes were in some respects (important though limited) more gifted by God and had a

mission to save the world. (See Wilson Jeremiah Moses, *Black Messiahs and Uncle Toms: Social and Literary Manipulation of a Religious Myth* [Philadelphia: Pennsylvania State University Press, 1982], 227 particularly.) Black leaders of her time accepted her, faults and all, as a friend with good intentions.

15. Many twentieth-century readers—not all of them women—respond to *UTC* as a book in praise of womanhood. As one scholar states, "In *Uncle Tom's Cabin* racial categories are subsumed by those of gender" (Amy Schrager Lang, *Prophetic Woman: Anne Hutchinson and the Problem of Dissent in the Literature of New England* [Berkeley, Los Angeles, London: University of California Press, 1987], 206. "Feel Right and Pray," a chapter on Stowe (193–214), emphasizes the exaltation of femininity in *UTC*.

16. Speaking personally, I find *UTC* not only fascinating but also different in kind from her later novels. Each of them was about characters, places, incidents, and subjects exactly as announced—Dr. Samuel Hopkins in New England, Harry Henderson in New York, etc. HBS wrote these books consciously as books. *UTC* is different, as she knew; she even claimed that God was the author. Perhaps so, but my conviction is that the HBS who poured herself into the story was a different HBS from the famous author of the completed *UTC*. Thus my particular fascination with the book does not lie in reading it as a sentimental novel, a purpose novel, or a religious novel (each of which it is), but in following it as an allegorical or symbolic success story.

Chapter Four

1. *A Key to "Uncle Tom's Cabin"* (Boston: John P. Jewett, 1853). Hereafter cited in the text as *Key*.

2. The London *Times* review (3 September 1852) was reprinted in New York as a pamphlet and also in the *National Anti-Slavery Standard,* 30 September 1852. It has recently been reprinted in Elizabeth Ammons's *Critical Essays on Harriet Beecher Stowe* (Boston: G.K. Hall, 1980), 25–34, along with the equally damning review from the *Southern Literary Messenger,* 7–24, to give balance to the eulogy by George Sand, 3–6. See Gossett, *"Uncle Tom's Cabin" and American Culture,* chapters 10–13, pp. 164–259, for a full account of the reception of *UTC* abroad as well as at home, North and South. Frank Luther Mott gives a graphic account of the excitement over the publication of *UTC* as reflected in the magazines (*A History of American Magazines,* vol. 2 [Cambridge, Mass.: Harvard University Press] 142–44).

3. William J. Grayson, "The Hireling and the Slave" (1854), as quoted by Vernon Louis Parrington, in *Main Currents in American Thought* (New York: Harcourt, Brace, 1927–30), vol. 2, 107. See also Jay B. Hubbell, *The South in American Literature 1607–1900* (Durham, N.C.: Duke University Press, 1954), 445–46.

4. James C. Derby, *Fifty Years among Authors, Books, and Publishers*

(New York: G.W. Carleton, 1884), 520–21. The amanuensis was presumably either Eliza or Harriet, both of whom served as their mother's secretaries throughout the rest of her life.

5. Stowe's pessimism regarding emancipation can be seen in a reference from *Dred* vol. 2, 212); in her phrase "*Utopian dream*" (preface to 1878 *Uncle Tom's Cabin*, xxxi); and in the explicit statement of McCray, "Mrs. Stowe never expected to see the slaves free" (Florine Thayer McCray, *The Life-Work of the Author of "Uncle Tom's Cabin"* [New York: Funk and Wagnalls, 1889], 102; hereafter cited in the text and notes as McCray).

6. Leslie A. Fiedler, who lavishes praise on *UTC* as "majority" literature, condemns *Dred* as "a failure—mythologically inert, structurally confused, moving to no one" (*The Inadvertent Epic* [New York: Simon & Schuster, 1979], 38, 83). Ellen Moers writes about *Dred* at length and with more sympathy in "Mrs. Stowe's Vengeance" (*New York Review of Books* 15 [3 September 1970]: 25–32), emphasizing that Stowe's tone is more belligerent than in *UTC*. Theodore R. Hovet also has some good words for the intellectual qualities of *Dred* in "Christian Revolution: Harriet Beecher Stowe's Response to Slavery and the Civil War" (*New England Quarterly* 47 [1974]: 535—49). As he shows, in 1856 she was extremely pessimistic about the prospects for reform.

7. *Sunny Memories of Foreign Lands* (Boston: Phillips, Sampson, 1854); the characteristic phrases quoted in this paragraph appear in vol. 2, 160, 332, and 228.

8. John Ruskin, *Letters of John Ruskin to Charles Eliot Norton* (Boston: Houghton, Mifflin, 1904), vol. 1, 54. Macaulay was roused to fury by her misrepresentation of his conversation in *Sunny Memories*. "A mighty foolish, impertinent book. . . . What blunders she makes. . . . She cannot even see. . . . I am glad that I met her so seldom, and sorry that I met her at all" (G. Otto Trevelyan, *Life and Letters of Lord Macaulay* [New York: Longmans, Green, reprint of 1875 edition], vol. 2, 302).

9. "Appeal to the Women of England" was favorably received by the British public. According to Frank J. Klingberg, "Harriet Beecher Stowe and Social Reform in England," in *American Historical Review* 43 (1938), 542–52, Stowe's three visits to England were all highly successful. Another historian has speculated that her initial popularity there was due partly to the value of *Uncle Tom's Cabin* as anti-American propaganda (Ephraim Douglass Adams, *Great Britain and the American Civil War* [New York: Russell and Russell, 1958], vol. 1, 33). The fullest treatment of the reception of Stowe's "Appeal" in the British press is Wendy F. Haman's article in the *New England Quarterly* 41 (1988), 3–24, "No Voice from England: Mrs. Stowe, Mr. Lincoln, and the British in the Civil War."

10. Stowe and Senator Sumner had been friends for years. No praise from her could have equaled in eloquence his tribute to *UTC* in his great speech of 26

August 1852 against the Fugitive Slave Act. "Behold a new and heavenly ally. A woman, inspired by Christian genius, enters the lists, like another Joan of Arc, and with marvellous power sweeps the popular heart. Now melting to tears, and now inspiring to rage, her work everywhere touches the conscience, and makes the Slave-Hunter more hateful (Charles Sumner, *Complete Works* [Boston: Lee and Shepard, 1900], vol. 3, 413–14). Forrest Wilson suspected that the atrocious attack on Sumner importantly influenced the shaping of *Dred*.

Chapter Five

1. *Religious Studies, Sketches, and Poems* (Boston: Houghton, Mifflin, 1896), 111. Hereafter cited in the text as *RS*.
2. McCray (416) describes *Woman in Sacred History* (New York: J. B. Ford, 1873; hereafter cited in the text as *WSH*) as "a superb volume which, in its plainest binding, sold for six dollars." It was issued in several forms, with poems and more chromos added, and sold in all about 50,000 copies (416–17). *Footsteps of the Master* lacked the lavish format, but it was reissued as part of *Religious Studies* and as vol. 15 of the collected *Writings*. *Woman in Sacred History* and *Footsteps of the Master* were originally articles in the *Christian Union*.
3. The entire composition was printed in Charles Edward Stowe's biography of his mother, 15–21, and has been reprinted in later biographies.
4. The historian Page Smith has said that *The American Woman's Home* (New York: J. B. Ford and Co., 1869) is "the classic nineteenth-century manual on housekeeping" and "certainly one of the most influential books of the age" (*Daughters of the Promised Land: Women in American History* [Boston: Little, Brown & Co., 1970], 205–6). If true, most of the credit is due Catherine.
5. The company failed because, according to John Raymond Howard, a member of the firm, it overstocked Beecher books when the Beecher-Tilton scandal knocked the bottom out of the market. (Howard, *Remembrance of Things Past*, [New York: T. Y. Crowell Co., 1925], 306.)
6. *My Wife and I; or, Harry Henderson's History* (New York: J. B. Ford, 1871), 49, 51, 63, 69, 80, 81, 149, 254, 328, 421.
7. Margaret Wyman made the plausible suggestion that Stowe's skepticism regarding woman suffrage, which is not observable in the December 1870 installment of the serial, was her shocked reaction to the free-love agitation of Victoria Woodhull, which received unfavorable publicity in January 1871. ("Harriet Beecher Stowe's Topical Novel on Woman Suffrage," *New England Quarterly* 25 [1952], 383–91.) This contradiction in Stowe's thinking, whatever its immediate cause, is not without parallel in her other works.
8. *We and Our Neighbors: Records of an Unfashionable Street* (New York: J. B. Ford, 1875), 48, 92, 95, 98, 147, 306, 342.
9. *Pink and White Tyranny: A Society Novel* (Boston: Roberts Brothers, 1871), 7, 27, 45; hereafter cited in the text as *PWT*. William Dean Howells,

who reviewed the book (anonymously) in the *Atlantic Monthly* (28 [September 1871], 377–78) classified it as a sermon. "Mrs. Stowe could not make a dull or meaningless sermon," he averred gallantly, then added that it was one "which we should commend more for the good purpose characteristic of it all, than for its strength of exegesis or for the dramatic impersonation of its ideas."

10. A troublesome minor question that biographers should consider is the possible instigation of her strong anti-Gallic sentiment at this time, which is not characteristic of her normal belief. She could read French well; on one of her European trips she had taken lessons to improve her pronunciation; and she had sent her daughters to Paris for their education. Nevertheless, for some reason, she worried throughout *Pink and White Tyranny* over the baleful French influence on American family life.

11. Few if any good words have been spoken for many years of the three society novels. They fared a little better when they were new. An anonymous reviewer of *My Wife and I,* the best of the three, after carefully balancing the pros and cons in *Harper's Magazine* (44 [1871–72]: 462–63), decided that it is "courageous and outspoken, and in its whole moral tone and atmosphere is high and noble, far more so than most modern romances." Milton Rugoff stated in *The Beechers* (536) that it was popular, doubling the circulation of the *Christian Union* and selling 50,000 as a hardcover book. Alice Crozier (*The Novels of Harriet Beecher Stowe* [New York: Oxford University Press, 1969]), like other later critics, found no good words for *Pink and White Tyranny,* "a novel always on the verge of turning into a lecture," but saw the other two novels as in some ways similar to the work of Howells; and Stowe herself regarded the three works as "true pictures of real life" (Crozier, *Novels,* 180). Paul John Eakin, in *The New England Girl: Cultural Ideals in Hawthorne, Stowe, Howells, and James* (Athens: University of Georgia Press, 1976), 232, found that Lillie Ellis, the central character of *Pink and White Tyranny,* is an anti-heroine revealing "the bankruptcy of this representative of contemporary girl-hood" in contrast to the Puritan maiden of the past. Dorothy Berkson's thoughtful article in Ammons's, "Millenial Politics and the Feminine Fiction of Harriet Beecher Stowe," 244–58, explains the antifeminism of the society novels as Stowe's repugnance at radical feminism: she still preferred the "true woman" type of her childhood to the aggressive independent "new woman." Margaret Marsh effectively cites *My Wife and I* for its documentary value as an expression of opinions liberal for the 1870s ("Suburban Men and Masculine Domesticity, 1870–1915," in *American Quarterly* 40 [1988] 165–86; see references on 169, 171, 173).

12. *The Chimney-Corner* (Boston: Ticknor & Fields, 1868), 55.

13. *House and Home Papers* (Boston: Ticknor & Fields, 1865), 110. The italics are hers. Forrest Wilson noted (496) that *House and Home Papers* were not as dull in the *Atlantic* as they are now, since "they had much of the flavor of the *Autocrat*" applied to the new subject of home beautification.

14. *The Chimney-Corner,* 22. The italics are hers.

15. A letter (number 5) in the Fields collection (Huntington Library, San Marino, Calif.) mentions her price for the *Atlantic* articles as $200 each. In her apprenticeship, before *UTC,* she had proudly claimed the ability to earn $400 a year from her writing (AF, 132).

Chapter Six

1. The authorship of the *First Geography for Children* is not clear. The book is a revision of the 1833 *Primary Geography for Children* (Cincinnati, Corey and Fairbank) by C. and H. Beecher. Harriet is believed to have written the original book, though Catherine, as the dominating senior educator, took chief credit. The revised version was made by either Catherine or Harriet—I hope by Catherine, as it is dangerously biased and bigoted, and writers about HBS have been saved embarrassment by ignoring it. Speculation has it (see Forrest Wilson, 406) that the 1855 revision was Catherine's work, although only Harriet—by then a famous writer—was named as author, to stimulate sales. For other plausible surmises about the 1833 book, see Wilson, 112. I hold HBS responsible for the views in the passages I quote, whether she wrote them or acquiesced in them.

2. *Oldtown Folks* (Boston: Fields, Osgood, 1869), 229; hereafter cited in the text as *OF.* More eulogistic, but difficult to quote briefly, are the passages on Mather on 285–86, 328–29.

3. Cotton Mather, *The Wonders of the Invisible World* (London: J.R. Smith Library of Old Authors Series, 1862 ed.), 12.

4. *Sam Lawson's Oldtown Fireside Stories,* (Boston: J. R. Osgood, 1872), 48. Hereafter cited in the text as *OFS.*

5. *Poganuc People: Their Loves and Lives* (New York: Fords, Howard, and Hulbert, 1878), 226. Hereafter cited in the text as *PP.*

6. Ibid., 308. For the greater religious power of women over male preachers see also *The Minister's Wooing,* 37, and "The Minister's Housekeeper," in *Oldtown Fireside Stories.*

7. Perry D. Westbrook views *Poganuc People* with more than usual favor; as Stowe's final view of New England it is "positive" and "more compact in structure and readable in style" than the earlier novels (*The New England Town in Fact and Fiction* [New York: Fairleigh Dickinson University Press, 1982], 108. He commends the character of farmer Zeph Higgins. "For plain 'sotness' and 'cussedness' he has no equal in American literature; yet he is as natural an outcropping of the New England hills as one of the immovable boulders in his own fields" (*Acres of Flint: Writers of Rural New England, 1870–1900* [Washington: Scarecrow Press, 1951], 87).

8. Sarah Orne Jewett, *Letters of Sarah Orne Jewett,* ed. Annie Fields (Boston: Houghton, Mifflin, 1911), 47. Jewett's admiration links Stowe to the

post–Civil War local-color vogue. Josephine Donovan's book is informative on this subject ("Harriet Beecher Stowe and the Emergence of a Female Arcadia," chapter 4, 50–67, (in *New England Local Color Literature: A Women's Tradition*.) Yet the distinction between regional and local-color literature is worth keeping, regional being the broader term. Stowe was regional in the main, from "A New England Tale" (1834) through *Poganuc People* (1878). *Sam Lawson's Oldtown Fireside Stories* (1872) is Stowe's contribution to the local-color movement; but "Deacon Pitkin's Farm" (1875), a rambling New England story for the *Christian Union*, rich in atmosphere and typical characters, is regional.

9. *The Pearl of Orr's Island: A Story of the Coast of Maine* (Boston: Ticknor and Fields, 1862), 396, 75, 45; hereafter cited in the text as *POI*. The Stowes' son Henry had recently died.

10. *The Minister's Wooing* (New York: Derby and Jackson, 1859), 458. Hereafter cited in the text as *MW*.

11. Ibid., 567. The italics are Stowe's.

12. McCray (281) quotes Dr. Park's statement. Calvin Stowe also unsuccessfully urged changes in the theological references (Charles Edward Stowe and Lyman Beecher Stowe, *Harriet Beecher Stowe: The Story of Her Life* [Boston: Houghton, Mifflin, 1911], 250). Charles H. Foster, in *The Rungless Ladder*, gives a clear account of the departures from biographical truth, with an explanation of the probable personal reasons for them (*The Rungless Ladder*, 87–90). How important are such inaccuracies in the novel? Christopher P. Wilson pays close attention to its "pragmatic and secularizing" aspect in "Tempests and Teapots: Harriet Beecher Stowe's *The Minister's Wooing*," *New England Quarterly* 58 (1985): 554–77. A valuable technical article by Lawrence Buell, "Calvinism Romanticized: Harriet Beecher Stowe, Samuel Hopkins, and *The Minister's Wooing*" (1978), reprinted in Ammons's *Critical Essays on Stowe*, 259–75, reveals Stowe's research efforts to present Hopkins's doctrines accurately. The plot is of course "almost total fabrication" and the characterization is sentimental; but the "religious climate" is reproduced accurately and parts of the dialogue are direct quotations from writings by Hopkins. In Buell's important book, *New England Literary Culture* (New York: Cambridge University Press, 1986), he makes a detailed and illuminating comparison of *The Minister's Wooing* and Hawthorne's *The Scarlet Letter* as major religious texts by the two "by far the most ambitious and distinguished literary chroniclers of New England history" (261). The entire chapter is notable, "Hawthorne and Stowe as Rival Interpreters of New England Puritanism," (261–80).

13. This preference for *Oldtown Folks* has not been unanimous. McCray, for one, discussed *The Minister's Wooing* with unsurpassable enthusiasm. Later readers, with less enthusiasm (rejecting *Oldtown Folks* as a novel, because of its shapelessness or its discursiveness), prefer *The Minister's Wooing* as a more acceptable taste of Stowe's New England. (See Alexander Cowie, *The Rise of the American Novel* [New York: American Book Co., 1948], 463, 455.) Although

the lengthy expositions of New England theology in *Oldtown Folks* have repelled some readers, they probably represent Stowe's greatest achievement as an interpreter of American life. Her insight into New England preachers, particularly the conservative types, is vouched for by many authorities, including Austin Warren (*New England Saints* [Ann Arbor: University of Michigan Press, 1956], 23–24, 32–33, 184). Her mature approach to the subject is shown as early as 1858. "It is a mark of a shallow mind to scorn these theological wrestlings and surgings; they have had in them something even sublime" (*Atlantic Monthly* 1 [1858]: 478). Some later critics also have found special merit in *The Minister's Wooing*. Paul John Eakin studies the Puritan maiden heroine and analyzes the novel in detail (*The New England Girl,* 28–44). Leo F. O'Connor writes about *The Minister's Wooing* in a section of his book, *Religion in the American Novel: The Search for Belief, 1860–1920* (Lanham, Md.: University Press of America, 1984), 36–46; the discussion is mainly about Hopkins, highlighting his confrontation with Simon Brown over slavery.

The curious may find interest in a little story for children, "The Minister's Watermelons." In it William Somers, an academy boy, tells how he fell in love with fellow student Lucy Sewell; and, under the domination of an older boy, Elliot Winton, stole her father's melons and confessed his fault. The psychological relationship is a repetition of that in *Oldtown Folks* between Horace, Tina, and the Byronic Ellery Davenport.

14. *Agnes of Sorrento* (Boston: Ticknor & Fields, 1862). Hereafter cited in the text as *AS*.

15. The italics appear in the original.

16. A more sympathetic analysis of *Agnes of Sorrento* is given by Nathalia Wright in *American Novelists in Italy* (Philadelphia: University of Pennsylvania Press, 1965), 88–103.

17. The quoted phrases in this paragraph are taken from HBS's correspondence, Fields, 304, 381.

18. Later accounts of the trial have been anti-Beecher. A particularly lively one, based on the court records and contemporary news stories, is by Robert Shaplen, *Free Love and Heavenly Sinners: The Story of the Great Henry Ward Beecher Scandal* (New York: Knopf, 1954).

19. *Palmetto-Leaves* (Boston, J. R. Osgood, 1873), 113, 138. Hereafter cited in the text as *PL*.

20. Stowe's life in Florida is best described in the local history by Mary B. Graff, *Mandarin on the St. Johns* (Gainesville, FL.: University of Florida Press, 1953), 47–85. Much earlier, however, Sidney Lanier had remarked that Mandarin's principal celebrity was Stowe's home.

Chapter Seven

1. *Independent,* 21 February 1856.
2. *Independent,* 15 November 1860.

3. See E. Bruce Kirkham, "The Writing of Harriet Beecher Stowe's *The Pearl of Orr's Island*" (*Colby Library Quarterly* 16 [1980]: 158–65), for bibliographical details.

4. Howard, *Remembrance of Things Past,* (New York: T. Y. Crowell Co., 1925), 215–18.

5. Ibid., 306.

6. Stowe's interest in psychic phenomena was not exclusively literary. She experimented with planchette (a device similar to the Ouija board) and contemplated preparing an article on it for the *Atlantic* (AF, 315–16). The messages she received are referred to by Howard Kerr in *Mediums and Spirit Rappers, and Roaring Radicals* (Urbana, 1972), 110. Stowe's account, as printed in her brother Charles's *Spiritual Manifestations* (Boston: Lee and Shepard, 1879), 25–36, is more remarkable for the sources of her information than for the messages received. The duchess of Sutherland was involved, and Charlotte Brontë communicated that she and Emily were at peace and that "Thackeray is very happy now" (31).

7. An account of *Old and New* can be found in Edward E. Hale, Jr.'s *Life and Letters of Edward Everett Hale* (Boston: Little, Brown & Co., 1917), vol. 2, 97–119. See also John R. Adams, *Edward Everett Hale* (Boston: Twayne, 1977), 80–82.

8. Stowe's association was probably the idea of her sister Isabelle, a radical feminist. See Rugoff, *The Beechers,* 431–33.

9. Robert Meredith (*The Politics of the Universe* [Nashville: Vanderbilt University Press, 1968], 187–88) mentions the *Congregationalist* of Boston as a magazine that listed her as a "special contributor," but no writings by her have been identified.

Chapter Eight

1. In 1886 she wrote, for her son's biography of her, that in her girlhood "I was very much interested in poetry, and it was my dream to be a poet." (Charles Edward Stowe, 32; Fields, 43; Forrest Wilson, 69.) She continued working in verse and produced a number of respectable religious lyrics and hymns.

2. Forrest Wilson, 209; Rugoff, *The Beechers,* 235.

3. *A Library of Famous Fiction* (New York: J. B. Ford, 1873), viii. Hereafter cited in the text as *LFF*.

4. On *Pilgrim's Progress:* "The loveliest and richest specimen of pure, tender, homely Saxon English which is to be found in any book *except* the Bible" (ibid., ix; italics by HBS). References to Bunyan's book occur in most of her novels, including *UTC, The Minister's Wooing,* and *Oldtown Folks.* For unfamiliar passages praising Bunyan, see her articles in *Hearth and Home,* 23 January 1869, and the *Christian Union,* 1 January 1873.

5. This magazine article, "The True Story of Lady Byron's Life," (*Atlantic Monthly* 24 [September 1869], 295–313), one of the most discussed of the century, reduced the circulation of the *Atlantic* from 50,000 to 35,000. Nevertheless it was also hailed, as by the *Nation*, as "one of the greatest successes ever achieved in any country" (Mott, *American Magazines,* vol. 2, 505). Stowe received much unfavorable criticism, and even trashy sensational magazines had a chance to express their shock, real or imagined, at finding such a scandalous article written by a woman for the staid *Atlantic*. (Mary Noel, *Villains Galore: The Hey-day of the Popular Story Weekly* [New York: Macmillan, 1954], 302–3.)

6. A summary of this controversy, with an extensive bibliography, is in Samuel C. Chew, *Byron in England* (New York: Charles Scribner's Sons, 1924), 278–83. Ethel Colburn Mayne, in *Byron,* 2nd ed. (New York: Charles Scribner's Sons, 1924), describes Stowe's book as a mixture of "invective and sanctification," a combination of carelessness, contradiction, and self-deception; and says that "never had truth so poor an advocate" (237, 446). Alice Crozier, who emphasizes the Byronic influence throughout her book, mentions lovers' quarrels, "protests of a betrayed lover, not a dispassionate critic" (*The Novels of Harriet Beecher Stowe* [1969], 212). In any case Forrest Wilson is on the right track, though flippant, in remarking about the book that followed the article, "a true title would be The Vindication of Harriet Beecher Stowe" (546).

7. Richard Croom Beatty, *Bayard Taylor: Laureate of the Gilded Age* (Norman: University of Oklahoma Press, 1936), 266.

8. The best account of *Cleon,* with the most extracts from the play, is in Fields, 43–49.

9. John T. Morse, Jr., *Life and Letters of Oliver Wendell Holmes* (Boston: Houghton, Mifflin, 1896), vol. 2, 179. The italics are Holmes's.

10. Henry Adams, *Letters of Henry Adams* (Boston: Houghton, Mifflin, 1930), 168.

11. In an *Atlantic* tribute to the duchess of Sutherland. See Ellen Moers, "The Myth of Corinne," chapter 9, 173–210, in *Literary Women* (New York: Doubleday & Co., 1976).

12. These feats are noted in the biographies. On her verbal memory of Scott's verse see Lyman Beecher Stowe, *Saints, Sinners,* 229; on the repetitive reading of *Ivanhoe,* see HBS, "Answer to Correspondence," *Hearth and Home,* 13 February 1869.

13. In *Queer Little People* (Boston: Ticknor & Fields, 1867), 173. See also "Literary Epidemics," *Evangelist,* 28 July 1842, and *Poganuc People* (1878), 131–32.

14. The details in this paragraph are assembled mainly from *Sunny Memories,* vol. 1, 195–220. In other places HBS misquotes familiar lines and makes a common error in giving the name of Shakespeare's son (vol. 2, 104; vol. 1,

150, 211). She was convinced that Shakespeare's mother was the original model for Desdemona (vol. 1, 203).

15. Professor Calvin Stowe's knowledge of biblical texts surpassed Harriet's; he was the thorough scholar, she the gifted amateur with a wonderful memory. Calvin's book, *Origin and History of the Books of the Bible* (Hartford: Hartford Publishing Co., 1867), is impressive in its detail and for the breadth of illustration. His objection to Hegelian theologians (253–312) is possibly narrow, but he frequently shows a cultural cosmopolitanism, as in a section on Matthew (152–54). "An examination of the Gospel of Matthew will show that it is constructed on a plan very similar to that of Xenophon's *Memorabilia of Socrates*" (153).

16. These casual references follow the course of European literature from Homer, Aeschylus, and Plato, through Virgil (quoted in Latin), Augustine, Tertullian, Dante, and Tasso, to Bossuet's sermons, Fénelon, and Chateaubriand. They also outline, selectively, English literary history beginning with Donne ("one might almost say her body thought") and continuing through Locke, Defoe, Addison, Pope, Dr. Johnson (his prayers), Gray, Goldsmith, Hannah More, Jane Porter, Coleridge, Thomas Moore, Carlyle, and Tennyson.

17. Also, "In the strictest New England times *Sir Charles Grandison* was often recommended by clergymen, and lay on the toilet-table of godly young women" (*Library of Famous Fiction*, vii).

18. Fields, 169. Although HBS read more than an afternoon's "great deal" of Goethe's *Faust,* she did not hesitate to tackle a complete synopsis in two paragraphs for *Woman in Sacred History* (304). A more personal reference to the "great poem" in *Footsteps of the Master* (*RS,* 93–94) is a tribute to the purified Margaret who "like a tender mother" saves the soul of the dying Faust in his "infantine weakness." HBS approved of the "wonderful mind" that recognized that even a fallen woman embodies "the eternal womanly [that] draws us upward and onward."

19. Fields, 317, 342. See also articles by HBS in *Hearth and Home,* January 1869. Even so, she wrote Fields, "Hawthorne ought to have lived in an orange grove in Florida" (AF, 343).

20. "A Dog's Mission," first published in *Youth's Companion* 53 (May 1880). A full and astute discussion of their friendship can be found in Kenny Ralph Marotta, "The Literary Relationship of George Eliot and Harriet Beecher Stowe," Ph. D. diss., Johns Hopkins University, 1974. Stowe had been brought up to regard another Victorian novelist, Charles Dickens, with suspicion. See "Literary Epidemics—No. 2," in the *Evangelist,* 13 July 1843, where she wittily attacks him as a poor moral influence. Among novels of social reform, she preferred Charles Kingsley's *Alton Locke* (1850) to anything she had read by Dickens (Forrest Wilson, *Crusader in Crinoline,* 427).

21. Lowell was not completely frank with Stowe. After the Byron article, he wrote, but not to her, that her good intentions had not produced a

good result, and that her evidence was unconvincing. (Lowell, *New Letters,* ed. M. A. DeWolfe Howe [New York: Harper & Brothers, 1932], 146.)

22. Samuel T. Pickard, *Life and Letters of John Greenleaf Whittier* (Boston: Houghton, Mifflin, 1895), vol. 2, 419.

23. Charles Eliot Norton, *Letters of Charles Eliot Norton* (Boston: Houghton, Mifflin, 1913), vol. 1, 186. This practice was not followed. Norton's own attitude toward Stowe was entirely friendly (vol. 1, 164).

24. Thomas Wentworth Higginson, *Cheerful Yesterdays* (Boston: Houghton Mifflin, 1898), 176–80. H. W. Longfellow also refers to this dinner, but without Higginson's wit (Samuel Longfellow, *Life of Henry Wadsworth Longfellow* [Boston: Houghton, Mifflin, 1899], vol. 2, 387). Stowe's skirmishes with alcohol amused even her friends. Mrs. Thomas Bailey Aldrich tells of accidentally getting her dead drunk (*Crowded Memories* [Boston: Houghton, Mifflin, 1919], 120–26). Contrary to the impression they made on the public, the Stowes were not total abstainers. Harriet was not averse to "very choice old Burgundy" taken regularly in the morning as a tonic; Calvin favored brandy, which Harriet also used as medicine. See references to alcohol in James C. Derby, *Fifty years among Authors, Books, and Publishers,* 521; Forrest Wilson, 416–17; Rugoff, *The Beechers,* 336. Wagenknecht tells the story in full, in *Harriet Beecher Stowe: The Known and the Unknown,* 191–94.

25. See Moers, *Literary Women,* 24–26.

26. On Bret Harte, see Forrest Wilson, 557; on Cable, see Arlin Turner, *George W. Cable, a Biography* (Durham, N.C.: Duke University Press, 1956), 112.

27. Girand Chester, *Embattled Maiden: The Life of Anna Dickinson* (New York: Putnam, 1951), 106; *Nation* 7 (1868): 346–47; Rugoff, *The Beechers,* 423.

28. McCray's biography of HBS, advertisement following 440. HBS soon repudiated McCray, who had misused private information for a full biography. The book was straight eulogy, but the Stowes hated it because it competed with the CES authorized biography. Forrest Wilson gives the full details of the incident, 629–33.

29. Jewett, *Letters,* 47.

30. James T. Fields, *Yesterdays with Authors* (Boston: Houghton, Mifflin, 1871), 15.

31. Elizabeth Cady Stanton, *Eighty Years and More* (New York: European Publishing Co., 1898), 264.

32. Annie Fields, 315, 313. In a similar vein, letter number 7 in the Fields collection (Huntington Library, San Marino, Calif.) mentions a "critical revision" of her poems.

33. By today's standards she need not have been ashamed—whenever she wrote carefully. Several letters in the Fields collection of the Huntington Library (number 10, 18, etc.) concern suitable copyreaders to correct her style. Among

other grammatical errors, she never mastered the schoolboy's demon—the mysterious "dangling participle." In the *Key to "Uncle Tom's Cabin,"* the first offense stands out on the first page of the preface.

34. Howells, *Literary Friends and Acquaintance* (New York: Harper & Brothers, 1901), 138–39. A later critic, Edmund Wilson, who does not let minor defects lessen his admiration for much of Stowe's writing, finds fault with her "verbosity" (*Patriotic Gore* [New York: Oxford University Press, 1962], 47); "she belongs to a school, or non-school, of loose writers," he states, stemming from Scott and including Cooper, an even worse writer (436). "She has no sense of proportion" and "flings out handfuls of words like confetti" (698).

35. HBS was not greedy but, being both generous and improvident, she was usually short of money. McCray, who as a poorly paid professional writer appears to have been unusually inquisitive about sales and prices, reported that *Sunny Memories* sold nearly 40,000 copies in Great Britain, and that American sales were unknown (223); that *Men of Our Times* sold nearly 40,000 copies (360) and that *Woman in Sacred History* sold "something like" 50,000 copies (417). HBS made over $20,000 on immediate profits from *Dred* and, as she told Fields, $11,500 on *The Minister's Wooing* as a book (Forrest Wilson, 531). The *Atlantic* paid $200 an installment for *Agnes of Sorrento,* and *Hearth and Home,* which never paid her, owed $5,000 for her year's contributions (Wilson, 464, 544). James Hart (*The Popular Book,* 112) states that "after 1853 any book [novel?] with her signature had a sure sale of at least 150,000 copies." One of her mass-production serials brought $8,000 for the newspaper rights (AF, 315).

Chapter Nine

1. Mark Twain, *Autobiography* (New York: Harper & Brothers, 1924), vol. 2, 243.

2. Daniel Dulany Addison, *Lucy Larcom: Life, Letters, and Diary* (Boston: Houghton, Mifflin, 1894), 146. Elizabeth Stuart Phelps tells similar stories in *Chapters of a Life* (Boston: Houghton, Mifflin, 1896), 134–37.

3. Howells, *Literary Friends,* 140.

4. *The Writings of Harriet Beecher Stowe,* Riverside ed. (Boston: Houghton, Miflin, 1896), vol. 15, 321.

5. Charles Edward Stowe's biography, inserted pages following the title page.

6. Barret Wendell, *Literary History of America* (New York: Charles Scribner's Sons, 1900), 354, 355, 356.

Selected Bibliography

Primary Sources

Harriet Beecher Stowe's stories and essays not reprinted from the original magazines or miscellaneous sources are identified in the text and notes.

Agnes of Sorrento. Boston: Ticknor and Fields, 1862.
The Chimney-Corner. By Christopher Crowfield. Boston: Ticknor and Fields, 1868.
Dred: A Tale of the Great Dismal Swamp. 2 vols. Boston: Phillips, Sampson, 1856.
First Geography for Children. Boston: Phillips, Sampson, 1855.
Footsteps of the Master. New York: J.B. Ford, 1877.
House and Home Papers. By Christopher Crowfield. Boston: Ticknor and Fields, 1865.
A Key to "Uncle Tom's Cabin." Boston: John P. Jewett, 1853.
Lady Byron Vindicated. Boston: Fields, Osgood, 1870.
A Library of Famous Fiction. New York: J. B. Ford, 1873.
Little Foxes. By Christopher Crowfield. Boston: Ticknor and Fields, 1866.
Little Pussy Willow. Boston: Fields, Osgood, 1870.
The Mayflower; or, Sketches of Scenes and Characters among the Descendants of the Puritans. New York: Harper and Brothers, 1843.
The May Flower, and Miscellaneous Writings. Boston: Phillips, Sampson, 1855.
Men of Our Times; or, Leading Patriots of the Day. Hartford: Hartford Publishing, 1868.
The Minister's Wooing. New York: Derby and Jackson, 1859.
My Wife and I; or, Harry Henderson's History. New York: J. B. Ford, 1871.
Oldtown Folks. Boston: Fields, Osgood, 1869.
Palmetto-Leaves. Boston: J. R. Osgood, 1873.
The Pearl of Orr's Island: A Story of the Coast of Maine. Boston: Ticknor and Fields, 1862.
Pink and White Tyranny: A Society Novel. Boston: Roberts Brothers, 1871.
Poganuc People: Their Loves and Lives. New York: Fords, Howard, and Hulbert, 1878.
Queer Little People. Boston: Ticknor and Fields, 1867.
Religious Studies, Sketches, and Poems. Boston: Houghton, Mifflin, 1896.
Sam Lawson's Oldtown Fireside Stories. Boston: J. R. Osgood, 1872.

Sunny Memories of Foreign Lands. 2 vols. Boston: Phillips, Sampson, 1854.
Uncle Tom's Cabin; or, Life among the Lowly. Boston: Houghton, Osgood, 1878.
This is a later edition, with extensive introductory matter. The first
edition, in two volumes, was published by John P. Jewett, 1852.
We and Our Neighbors: Records of an Unfashionable Street. New York: J. B. Ford,
1875.
Woman in Sacred History. New York: J. B. Ford, 1873.
The Writings of Harriet Beecher Stowe. Riverside ed. 16 vols. Boston: Houghton,
Mifflin, 1896.

Secondary Sources

Bibliographies

Ashton, Jean W. *Harriet Beecher Stowe: A Reference Guide.* Boston: G. K. Hall,
1977. An annotated list of writings about Stowe, chronologically arranged from 1843 to 1974. Includes reviews, essays, and books, with
numerous quotations, some of which are quaint or surprising. Well
indexed.
Hildreth, Margaret Holbrook. *Harriet Beecher Stowe: A Bibliography.* Ham-
den, Conn.: Archon Books, Shoe String Press, 1976. A virtually complete and accurate checklist of Stowe's books and other published writings, including contributions to periodicals (approximately 150 pages).
Also about one hundred pages listing writing about her in books and
periodicals. A useful book for study but not a true bibliography for
collectors.

Biographies

Fields, Annie. *Life and Letters of Harriet Beecher Stowe.* Boston: Houghton,
Mifflin, 1898. Deeply and inherently sympathetic, by a personal friend
(from 1860) and professional associate who was also a celebrity in her own
right. For appreciation of Fields see M. A. DeWolfe Howe's book,
Memories of a Hostess (Boston, 1922) and Henry James's article, "Mr. and
Mrs. James T. Fields," *Atlantic Monthly* 116 [1915], 21–31.
Gilbertson, Catherine. *Harriet Beecher Stowe.* New York: D. Appleton-
Century, 1937. Nicely written and well informed, this book is one of
several that are intended to reach the so-called general public. Two others
serving the same purpose are Johanna Johnston's *Runaway to Heaven: The
Story of Harriet Beecher Stowe,* Garden City, N.Y.: Doubleday, 1963, and

Noel B. Gerson's *Harriet Beecher Stowe: A Biography*, New York: Praeger Publishers, 1976.

McCray, Florine Thayer. *The Life-Work of the Author of "Uncle Tom's Cabin."* New York: Funk and Wagnalls, 1889. This unauthorized book, planned as a magazine article, is expanded to 440 pages by the inclusion of long eulogistic summaries of some of Stowe's books.

Stowe, Charles Edward. *Life of Harriet Beecher Stowe Compiled from Her Letters and Journals.* Boston: Houghton, Mifflin, 1889. The authorized family biography. It contains the first printing of indispensable letters and other documents and is the foundation of all later biographies. Written by HBS's youngest child (born 1850), it tells the story of her life as she wished and had hoped to tell it herself as an autobiography. Two later books by members of the family add some new material: *Harriet Beecher Stowe: The Story of Her Life* (Boston: Houghton, Mifflin, 1911) by Charles Edward Stowe and Lyman Beecher Stowe; and *Saints, Sinners, and Beechers* (Indianapolis: Bobbs-Merrill, 1934) by Lyman Beecher Stowe.

Wagenknecht, Edward. *Harriet Beecher Stowe: The Known and the Unknown.* New York: Oxford University Press, 1965. As a synthesis of biography and literary criticism, this psychograph is probably the most accurate profile of Stowe's personal and literary character. A vast number of details arranged topically with chapters on Stowe as writer, reader, and reformer as well as daughter, wife, and mother.

Wilson, Forrest. *Crusader in Crinoline: The Life of Harriet Beecher Stowe.* Philadelphia: J. B. Lippincott, 1941. This book was awarded the Pulitzer Prize as the best biography of the year. It is much the most vivid and complete biography, sympathetic yet objective, with excellent documentation. Additional archival holdings not available to Wilson have been utilized by later writers, particularly Kathryn Kish Sklar, in *Catharine Beecher: A Study in American Domesticity* (New Haven: Yale University Press, 1973), and Milton Rugoff, *The Beechers: An American Family in the Nineteenth Century* (New York: Harper and Row, 1981).

Biographical Sketches

Anthony, Katharine. "Harriet Beecher Stowe." In *Dictionary of American Biography,* vol. 28. New York: Charles Scribner's Sons, 1936.

Bradford, Gamaliel. *Portraits of American Women.* Boston: Houghton, Mifflin, 1919.

Erskine, John. *Leading American Novelists.* New York: Henry Holt, 1910. Biographical and critical link between nineteenth- and twentieth-century evaluations.

Rourke, Constance M. *Trumpets of Jubilee.* New York: Harcourt, Brace, 1921. An intuitive, persuasive interpretation of Stowe's character in its cultural setting.

Studies

Ammons, Elizabeth, ed. *Critical Essays on Harriet Beecher Stowe*. Boston: G. K. Hall, 1980. Forty-four selections from 1852 to 1980, including important book reviews, reminiscences by friends, literary and historical appraisals, excerpts from books, and academic research articles. A good introduction to the study of Stowe's reputation. The same purpose is served on a smaller scale by the article on Stowe in *Nineteenth Century Literary Criticism* 3 (1983): 535–69, which reprints brief passages from forty-four sources, 1852–1974, and includes lists of additional primary and secondary sources of information.

Fiedler, Leslie A. *The Inadvertent Epic: From "Uncle Tom's Cabin" to "Roots."* New York: Simon and Schuster, 1979. Lively radio talks, in Fiedler's characteristic clever phrasing, on *UTC* and some twentieth-century derivatives. The principal subjects, all of which are directly or indirectly hostile to Stowe's portrayal of the South, are three novels by Thomas Dixon, the D. W. Griffith film *Birth of a Nation,* Margaret Mitchell's novel *Gone with the Wind,* and Alex Haley's *Roots.*

Foster, Charles H. *The Rungless Ladder: Harriet Beecher Stowe and New England Puritanism.* Durham, N.C.: Duke University Press, 1954. The basic authoritative exposition of the theological and religious elements in Stowe's novels. Gayle Kimball looks at the same subject from a woman's point of view in *The Religious Ideas of Harriet Beecher Stowe: The Gospel of Womanhood* (New York: Edward Mellon Press, 1983).

Gossett, Thomas F. *"Uncle Tom's Cabin" and American Culture*. Dallas: Southern Methodist University Press, 1985. This splendid big book is more than a history of America's most discussed novel; it also proves that the book deserves the attention it has received. The first section, about 80 pages, describes the conditions that led to the creation of the book. The second section, another 80 pages, is an elaborate analysis of the book as fiction and social criticism. The remaining 250 pages recount the immediate reception of the book in the North, the South, and in Europe; the replies; the dramatic versions; and the recent lively adverse criticism. Readable text, provocative notes, and extensive bibliography.

Kirkham, E. Bruce. *The Building of "Uncle Tom's Cabin."* Knoxville: University of Tennessee Press, 1977. An expert bibliographical account of the magazine publication and the first edition of the book, with valuable illustrations showing manuscript revisions. Contains some well-founded literary criticism and gives attention to Stowe's preparation for writing the book.

Moers, Ellen. *Harriet Beecher Stowe and American Literature.* Hartford: The Stowe-Day Foundation, 1978. A spirited lecture: "My intention is to put *UTC* back in American Literature where it belongs, for I think it is a great novel." This lecture does not repeat the many passages on

HBS in Moers's book *Literary Women,* Garden City, N.Y.: Doubleday, 1976.

Sundquist, Eric J., ed. *New Essays on "Uncle Tom's Cabin."* New York: Cambridge University Press, 1986. Six sophisticated, heavily annotated articles by research scholars on the sources and literary influence of the book, the characterization of women and of blacks, Stowe's use of the Gothic, and her religion. The editor provides a serious intellectual framework for the anthology. He is also one of the six writers about Stowe in the cooperative *Columbia Literary History of the United States* (New York: Columbia University Press, 1988).

Surveys of Stowe's Novels

Cowie, Alexander. *The Rise of the American Novel.* New York: American Book, 1948.

Hubbell, Jay B. *The South in American Literature, 1607–1900.* Durham, N.C.: Duke University Press, 1954.

Parrington, Vernon L. *Main Currents in American Thought.* vol. 2, *The Romantic Revolution in America.* New York: Harcourt, Brace, 1927.

Quinn, Arthur Hobson. *American Fiction, an Historical and Critical Survey.* New York: D. Appleton-Century, 1936.

Van Doren, Carl. *The American Novel, 1789–1939.* New York: Macmillan, 1940.

Wagenknecht, Edward. *Cavalcade of the American Novel.* New York: Henry Holt, 1952. An unusually comprehensive survey.

Whicher, George F. [Harriet Beecher Stowe], in *Literary History of the United States,* 581–86. New York: Macmillan, 1948.

Wilson, Edmund. *Patriotic Gore: Studies in the Literature of the American Civil War.* New York: Oxford University Press, 1962. A spirited and stimulating discussion, both biographical and critical, of Stowe and her husband.

Index